Conci
Inse
Guide

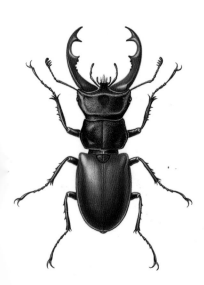

There are 47 individual Wildlife Trusts covering the whole of the UK and the Isle of Man and Alderney. Together The Wildlife Trusts are the largest UK voluntary organization dedicated to protecting wildlife and wild places everywhere – at land and sea. They are supported by 791,000 members, 150,000 of whom belong to their junior branch, Wildlife Watch. Every year The Wildlife Trusts work with thousands of schools, and their nature reserves and visitor centres receive millions of visitors.

The Wildlife Trusts work in partnership with hundreds of landowners and businesses across the UK in towns, cities and the wider countryside. Building on their existing network of 2,250 nature reserves, The Wildlife Trusts' recovery plan for the UK's wildlife and fragmented habitats, known as A Living Landscape, is being achieved through restoring, recreating and reconnecting large areas of wildlife habitat. As well as protecting wildlife this is helping to safeguard the ecosystems that we depend on for services like clean air and water.

The Wildlife Trusts are also working to protect the UK's marine environment. They are involved with many marine conservation projects around the UK, often surveying and collecting vital data on the state of our seas. Every year they run National Marine Week in August – a two-week celebration of our seas with hundreds of events taking place around the UK.

All 47 Wildlife Trusts are members of the Royal Society of Wildlife Trusts (Registered charity number 207238). To find your local Wildlife Trust visit wildlifetrusts.org

THE
wildlife
TRUSTS

Concise

Insect

Guide

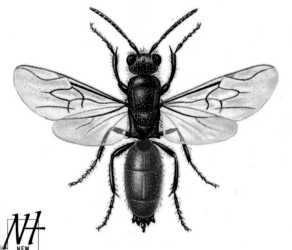

NH
NEW
HOLLAND

First published in 2011 by New Holland Publishers (UK) Ltd

London · Cape Town · Sydney · Auckland

www.newhollandpublishers.com

Garfield House, 86–88 Edgware Road, London W2 2EA, UK

80 McKenzie Street, Cape Town 8001, South Africa

Unit 1, 66 Gibbes Street, Chatswood, New South Wales 2067, Australia

218 Lake Road, Northcote, Auckland, New Zealand

10 9 8 7 6 5 4 3 2 1

ISBN 978 1 84773 604 8

Series Editor: Krystyna Mayer

Design: Alan Marshall

Illustrators: Sandra Doyle and Stuart Carter

Production: Melanie Dowland

Publisher: Simon Papps

Editorial Direction: Rosemary Wilkinson

Reproduction by Modern Age Repro Co. Ltd., Hong Kong

Printed and bound in China by Leo Paper Group

OTHER TITLES IN SERIES   *Concise Bird Guide*
Concise Butterfly & Moth Guide
Concise Wild Flower Guide
Concise Garden Wildlife Guide
Concise Tree Guide

Contents

Introduction

Insects are invertebrates, and thus have no internal skeleton. Instead they have an outer shell that contains the internal organs. They are distinguished from spiders and other arachnids by having six legs (arachnids have eight). During its lifetime an insect will go through a series of metamorphoses. At each of these stages it changes its appearance quite dramatically. About a million insect species have been identified so far, and more remain to be described. Almost 100,000 species are found in Europe, with more than 20,000 occurring in Britain. The *Concise Insect Guide* illustrates some of the most common and distinctive species, and provides details of their distinguishing characteristics, distribution, habitat and behaviour.

Insect Structure

Some insects are so small that a microscope is needed to see them clearly, while a number of moths and dragonflies have wingspans of up to 12cm. The form that they take is also very varied, but they do share certain anatomical characteristics. The bodies of adult insects have three main parts: the head, the thorax and the abdomen.

Head

The head has a pair of compound *eyes*, whose surfaces are faceted with tiny lenses. The number of these lenses, or facets, varies, but dragonflies, which are swift fliers and active predators, have several thousand in each eye, while some soil-dwelling insects may have none. In addition some insects have *ocelli*, very simple eyes on the front of the head, probably for detecting the intensity of light rather than for producing images. Insects have two *antennae*, which are the sensors of smell and touch. Some species have simple antennae that are a series of similar segments well supplied with nerve endings. In other species the antennae may be more complex: branched as in weevils or feather-shaped as in moths.

The head also contains the **mouthparts**, which are complex and vary according to the feeding method of a species. The mouthparts comprise a pair of jaws, a pair of secondary jaws and a lower lip. There are also four palps that examine the food before it is eaten. The secondary jaws and the lower lip hold the food steady, while the other set of jaws cuts it up. The mouthparts of species that feed on liquids have been modified quite dramatically. True bugs that feed on the sap of plants have piercing mouthparts. Mosquitoes and horseflies have long needle-like jaws, with which they pierce an animal's skin and withdraw its blood. Moths and butterflies have no jaws, but the secondary jaws have become linked together to form a long **proboscis**, through which they can suck nectar.

Thorax

The thorax is the motor centre of an insect. It has three segments, on each of which is a pair of legs. The **pronotum** is a tough plate over the front of the thorax. The **legs** are variable, but have a femur or thigh, a tibia or shin, and a tarsus or foot. The second segment carries a pair of

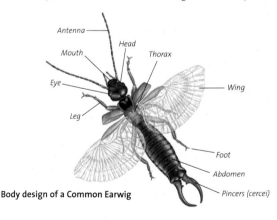

Body design of a Common Earwig

wings. If there is a second pair of wings, they are on the third segment. Most insects have wings, but they are missing from the primitive bristletails and springtails, and from the parasitic lice and fleas. The scientific names of many of the orders of insects describe their wings: Coleoptera (beetles) means 'leather wings', Lepidoptera (moths and butterflies) means 'scaly wings', Diptera (flies) means 'two wings'. The forewings of beetles (***elytra***) are thick and leathery, providing a covering for the hindwings. In flight they are held upright.

Abdomen

The abdomen is the centre of digestion and excretion. It is also where the sexual organs are situated. Most insects have eleven abdominal segments. At the tip there is a pair of ***cerci***, or tail-feelers. Earwig cerci consist of pincers that may be used in fighting, while those of many male bush-crickets and some other insects are used for grasping the female during mating. Females have an ***ovipositor*** between the eighth and ninth segments, usually concealed inside the body. Some species, such as the ichneumons and the Horntail, have long and exposed ovipositors. In bees and wasps, the ovipositor has lost its egg-laying function and has been replaced by a sting.

Life Cycles of Insects

It is well known that insects go through a series of developmental stages, or metamorphoses. However, the nature and timing of these stages differ between groups and species. The first stage is the egg. The hatchling from the egg looks nothing like its parent, except in the case of some of the most primitive insects. The best-known life cycle is that of butterflies, whose larvae are caterpillars, which then pupate to become chrysalids, from which emerge the adult insects. The caterpillar's sole purpose is eating, and as it grows it sheds its outer covering in a series of moults. As an insect moults it becomes slow and seeks cover because it is very vulnerable; the process of moulting is thus difficult to see in the wild. Dragonflies lay their eggs in water

The life cycle of the Stag Beetle

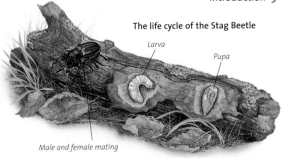

Larva

Pupa

Male and female mating

and the larvae develop underwater, emerging up the stems of plants, then shedding their larval casing to emerge as adult insects. Grasshoppers have a partial metamorphosis, with the young, or nymphs, looking like tiny adults and growing in a series of nymphal stages, shedding their skins several times until they reach adulthood.

Distinguishing Between Insects
The insects in this book appear within the orders to which they belong. They are briefly described below.

Thysanura/Bristletails Primitive wingless insects with three 'tails', each fringed with minute bristles, and tapering wedge-shaped bodies clothed with shiny scales. They are scavengers.

Ephemeroptera/Mayflies Delicate insects with 1–2 pairs of wings, and 2–3 slim filaments at the rear. Their nymphs live in water, and the adults do not feed. There are 51 mayfly species in Britain.

Odonata/Dragonflies & Damselflies These striking insects have large eyes that cover most of the head, four wings and a long body with 10 segments. Dragonflies rest with their wings at right angles to the thorax, while damselflies hold their wings closed over the abdomen. About 120 species breed in Europe, 38 of which breed in Britain.

Orthoptera/Grasshoppers & Crickets These insects produce a greater variety of sounds than any other insect order. All have strong hindlegs for jumping. There are about 250 species in Europe, with 30 in Britain.

Dermaptera/Earwigs Elongated insects with pincer-like cercei, which are longer and more curved in males than in females. They are nocturnal ground-living scavengers that eat both plant and animal matter, and hibernate during winter. Of the 1,300 known species, 34 occur in Europe, with 4 being found in Britain.

Dictyoptera/Cockroaches & Mantids Flattened fast-running insects with long antennae and bristly legs. There are about 3,500 species of cockroach worldwide, with 3 native to Britain. Of the world's 2,000 mantid species, 18 are found in southern and central Europe.

Psocoptera/Psocids Very small winged and wingless insects that are also known as booklice, barklice and dustlice. All have biting jaws. About 2,000 species have been described worldwide.

Hemiptera/True Bugs The shapes and sizes of bugs vary, but they all share a piercing beak, which they use to extract juices from animals and plants. There are roughly 75,000 species worldwide. In Europe there are 8,000, of which 1,700 are found in Britain and Ireland.

Thysanoptera/Thrips These are tiny and usually dark-coloured insects with two pairs of feathery wings. They are also known as thunder-flies because of their habit of flying in still, thundery weather. Females have curved ovipositors. More than 3,000 species are known.

Neuroptera/Lacewings These soft-bodied insects have large and flimsy wings. There are about 4,500 known species, of which around 60 are found in Britain.

Coleoptera/Beetles This is the largest insect order. The leathery casing (elytra) on the abdomen of a beetle comprises the forewings, which are held vertically in flight. Beetles are clumsy and distinctive when flying, but spend most of their time on the ground under stones and logs. There are more than 300,000 species worldwide, with over 20,000 in Europe, of which 4,000 occur in Britain.

Mecoptera/Scorpion Flies These are winged insects with distinctive 'beaks'. There are about 300 known species, of which only 4 are found in Britain.

Siphonaptera/Fleas These tiny wingless insects suck the blood of birds and mammals. They often breed on one host species, or a group of similar hosts. Their bodies are flattened to enable them to move through fur or feathers.

Diptera/True Flies Most true flies have only two wings, and adults feed on liquids. Some, like female horseflies and mosquitoes, suck blood, but most feed on other liquids such as nectar. There are almost 100,000 known species worldwide, with 5,200 in Britain.

Trichoptera/Caddis Flies Mainly brown insects with wings clothed with tiny hairs. Their larvae live in water, and many make portable protective cases from materials such as sand. There are almost 6,000 species worldwide, with 189 in Britain.

Lepidoptera/Butterflies & Moths There are more than 100,000 species of Lepidoptera worldwide, with 2,300 in Europe. A separate book in this series has been devoted to butterflies and moths, so they are not covered in this one.

Hymenoptera/Sawflies, Ichneumons, Ants, Wasps and Bees Insects in this very large order have four wings with relatively large cells, their hindwings being much smaller than their forewings. Most bees and wasps are solitary, but ants, some wasps, bumblebees and Honey Bees are social. There are more than 100,000 species worldwide, with over 300 in Britain.

Silverfish
Lepisma saccharina

SIZE AND DESCRIPTION Length 13mm. Fast-running wingless insect with three long tail-like appendages. Tapering body is covered in shiny silvery scales, which make it slippery and help it to escape from ants and spiders. The antennae are fine and the eyes are small.
HABITAT Houses and garden sheds, with damp places preferred. Common throughout Britain.
FOOD AND HABITS Nocturnal feeder that eats starchy material such as flour, paper and gum.

Firebrat
Thermobia domestica

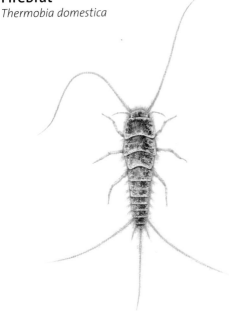

SIZE AND DESCRIPTION Length 13mm. Wingless insect with three long and bristly tails. Body is brown and tapering. Antennae are longer than those of Silverfish (opposite).

HABITAT Found indoors in warm places such as heating ducts. Often occurs in bakeries.

FOOD AND HABITS Feeds on starchy material such as flour.

Pond Olive
Cloeon dipterum

SIZE AND DESCRIPTION Length 7–11mm (body); 12–18mm (tails). Delicate insect with two tails, although many mayfly species have three tails. Also unlike other mayflies, which have two pairs of wings, the front of which are the largest, it has only one pair. Front edges of female's wings are brownish, while male has big eyes that are located higher than the rest of his head.

HABITAT Small areas of still water. Common in Britain and other parts of Europe.

FOOD AND HABITS Flies May–October. Mostly active at dawn and dusk, or at night. Adult mayflies do not feed, living only for a maximum of a few days, with some species living for less than an hour. Nymphs feed on algae.

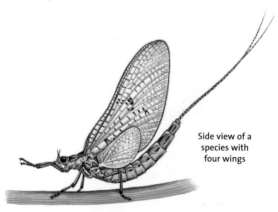

Side view of a species with four wings

A mayfly
nymph

Common Blue Damselfly
Enallagma cyathigerum

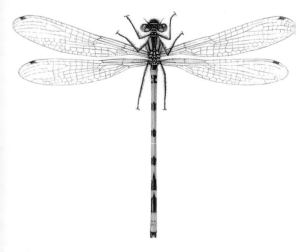

Size and description Length 29–36mm; hindwing 15–21mm. Male has a blue abdomen with black markings; segments 8–9 are all-blue. Female has a yellowish or bluish abdomen with variable dark markings. Strong flier.

Habitat A variety of inland water bodies, including ponds, gravel pits, lakes, slow rivers and canals, throughout Europe except Iceland, the Mediterranean islands, southern Italy and the Greek Peloponnese. One of the most common dragonflies.

Food and habits Flies May–September. Feeds on insects such as aphids. May pounce on dark spots on leaves, mistaking them for insects. Sometimes occurs in clusters of hundreds of individuals.

Blue-tailed Damselfly
Ischnura elegans

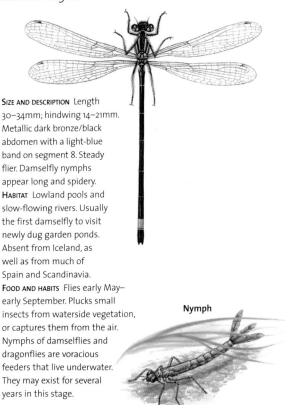

SIZE AND DESCRIPTION Length 30–34mm; hindwing 14–21mm. Metallic dark bronze/black abdomen with a light-blue band on segment 8. Steady flier. Damselfly nymphs appear long and spidery.

HABITAT Lowland pools and slow-flowing rivers. Usually the first damselfly to visit newly dug garden ponds. Absent from Iceland, as well as from much of Spain and Scandinavia.

FOOD AND HABITS Flies early May– early September. Plucks small insects from waterside vegetation, or captures them from the air. Nymphs of damselflies and dragonflies are voracious feeders that live underwater. They may exist for several years in this stage.

Nymph

Azure Damselfly
Coenagrion puella

Size and description Length 33–35mm; hindwing 15–24mm. Male has a blue abdomen with black markings and a totally blue eighth segment. Female has a dark abdomen with blue or green markings.

Habitat Prefers small sheltered ponds, including garden ponds, with emergent vegetation. Found from Ireland and southern Scotland across Europe, and south to North Africa. One of the most common damselflies.

Food and habits Flies mid-May–late August. Often seen in sunny meadows. Adults feed on small flying insects. Nymphs feed on small aquatic crustaceans and insects.

Large Red Damselfly
Pyrrhosoma nymphula

SIZE AND DESCRIPTION Length 33–36mm; hindwing 19–24mm. Red abdomen with black markings. There are three female forms, varying in the amount of black on the abdomen.

HABITAT Clear streams, ponds, lakes, ditches and canals across Europe except northern Scandinavia, Iceland and Sardinia. Widespread and common in Britain, although it has declined in the last 30 years in areas with intensive cultivation, particularly in eastern England.

FOOD AND HABITS Flies late April–late September, usually in large numbers. Rests on marginal plants. Feeds on small insects.

Banded Demoiselle
Calopteryx splendens

SIZE AND DESCRIPTION Length 45–48mm; hindwing 27–36mm. Wings of male each have a dark blue-black band across the centre. Female's wings are iridescent pale green. Body is metallic blue-green in male, green with a bronze tip in female. Fluttering butterfly-like flight.
HABITAT Slow-flowing lowland streams and rivers, particularly those with muddy bottoms. Occurs in most of Europe, except Scotland and

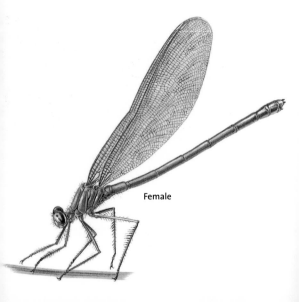

Female

northern Scandinavia. In England restricted to south of Blackpool and Middlesborough, with isolated populations in the Lake District. Occurs in most of Ireland. Like Beautiful Demoiselle (page 22), it is sensitive to pollution.

FOOD AND HABITS Flies early May–end August. Feeds on insects. Male often performs a fluttering display flight in front of females.

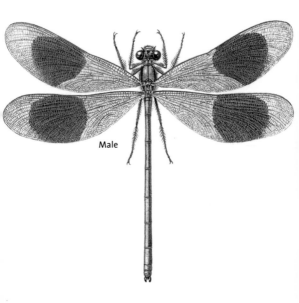

Male

Beautiful Demoiselle
Calopteryx virgo

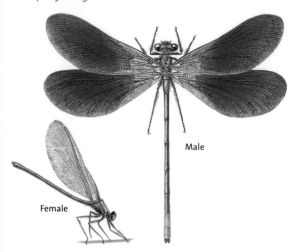

Male

Female

SIZE AND DESCRIPTION Length 45–49mm; hindwing 24–36mm. With Banded Demoiselle (page 20), the only damselfly species in Britain with obviously coloured wings. Male's wings are purplish blue-black, those of female iridescent brown-green. Body colour is metallic blue-green in male, and green with a bronze tip in female. Fluttering butterfly-like flight.

HABITAT Fast-flowing streams, particularly those with sand or gravel bottoms, often in heathland or moorland areas. Occasionally found in ponds. Widespread, but not found in far north. Common in many parts of continental Europe.

FOOD AND HABITS Flies late May–end August. Feeds on insects.

Brilliant Emerald
Somatochlora metallica

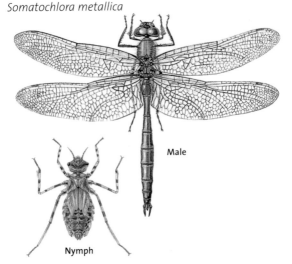

Male

Nymph

SIZE AND DESCRIPTION Length 50–55mm; hindwing 34–38mm. Dark
metallic emerald-green body with a bright bronze sheen. Eyes are
apple-green. Wings are suffused with saffron, particularly in female.
Male has a slightly club-shaped abdomen. Dragonfly nymphs are
shorter, stouter and often very much fatter than damselfly nymphs.
HABITAT Lowland marshes, fens and wet meadows, mainly in central
and northern Europe. Scarce in Britain, but locally common where it
occurs in the Scottish Highlands and south-east England. Threatened
by over-management or lack of appropriate management, deforesta-
tion, water-level reduction, pollution and the introduction of fish.
FOOD AND HABITS Flies June–mid-August. Feeds on insects.

Golden-ringed Dragonfly
Cordulegaster boltonii

SIZE AND DESCRIPTION Length 74–80mm (m), 80–85mm (f); hindwing 45–51mm. Striking black insect with yellow rings along the abdomen. Female is more parallel sided than male and has a very long ovipositor. Bright green eyes meet at a point on top of the head. One of the largest dragonflies in Britain.

HABITAT Acidic rivers and streams; also occurs on heathland. Found throughout Europe except far north. In Britain common on rivers in southern England, Wales, the Lake District and western Scotland.

FOOD AND HABITS Flies May–September. Feeds on insects. Breeds in relatively fast-flowing streams; female lays eggs in silt.

Emperor Dragonfly
Anax imperator

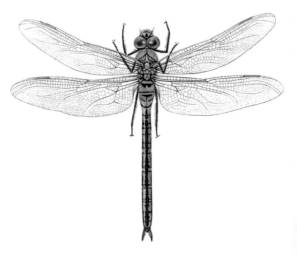

SIZE AND DESCRIPTION Length 66–84mm; hindwing 45–52mm. Male has greenish-blue eyes, an apple-green thorax and a bright blue abdomen with a thick black stripe down the back. Female is usually green, but may be blue. Males fly strongly, patrolling territory above human head height.

HABITAT Well-vegetated pools, ponds, ditches and slow-flowing rivers across Europe, southwards from Denmark. Known to visit woodland rides and glades when hunting.

FOOD AND HABITS Flies late May–mid-August. Hunts flies, moths and beetles, and even takes tadpoles from the water's surface.

Common Hawker

Aeshna juncea

Size and description Length 65–80mm; hindwing 40–48mm. Male has a black abdomen with blue spots and small yellow marks. Female is brown with yellow marks. Flies well and strongly – males spend long periods on the wing and rarely perch.

Habitat A variety of still waters, including lakes, ponds, peat bogs and still pools. Found south from northern Norway to the Pyrenees; absent from Iceland. Occurs at 800–1,000m in southern part of range.

Food and habits Flies late June–October. Hawks for other insects, often some way from water.

Southern Hawker
Aeshna cyanea

SIZE AND DESCRIPTION Length 67–76mm; hindwing 43–53mm. Male is dark with pairs of green markings on the first seven abdominal segments, and blue markings on segments 8–10. Female has green markings on her brown abdomen.

HABITAT Ponds, pools and lakes at up to 1,400m, and slow-flowing rivers. Widespread across Europe except far north.

FOOD AND HABITS Flies mid-June–October. Adults feed on flying insects. Nymphs eat aquatic insects, tadpoles and small fish. Males fly at human waist height and are inquisitive.

Brown Hawker
Aeshna grandis

SIZE AND DESCRIPTION Length 70–77mm; hindwing 41–49mm. Brown wings make this species unmistakable. Male has a brown abdomen with bright blue spots. Female has yellow markings on her brown abdomen. Both sexes have diagonal marks on the sides of the thorax. Strong flier. Males characteristically hover low down near human observers and observe them.

HABITAT Woodland ponds, lakes, canals, peat bogs and slow-flowing rivers. Absent from Iceland, Iberia, Italy, Greece and northern Scandinavia. Very common in lowland Wales and England, more local further north and with isolated populations in Scotland.

FOOD AND HABITS Flies mid-June–mid-October. Hunts flies, mosquitoes, moths and butterflies.

Migrant Hawker
Aeshna mixta

SIZE AND DESCRIPTION Length 56–64mm; hindwing 37–42mm. Dark brown and blue male has a bright blue spot on the side at the base of his abdomen. Brown female has small yellow spots. Neat, elegant and sometimes jerky flight.

HABITAT Still or slow-flowing water including ponds, gravel pits, lakes, canals and slow-running rivers. Distributed from England and Wales across Europe, south from the Baltic to North Africa. Until the 1940s, an uncommon migrant from southern Europe, but has gradually increased its range from a breeding population in south-east England, where it is now common. Migrations from the Continent increase British population in late summer.

FOOD AND HABITS Flies July–October. Feeds on insects. Approachable.

Four-spotted Chaser
Libellula quadrimaculata

Size and description Length 40–48mm; hindwing 32–40mm. Broad brown body with yellow patches along each side and black at the tip. Two dark marks on the leading edge of each wing.

Habitat Still water with plenty of vegetation. Found throughout Europe except Iceland. Widespread in Britain, but not found in many parts of north-east England.

Food and habits Flies mid-May–mid-August. Feeds on insects. Frequently perches in the open and flies out over the water. Aggressive and territorial nature.

Broad-bodied Chaser
Libellula depressa

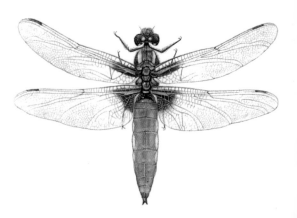

SIZE AND DESCRIPTION Length 39–48mm; hindwing 32–38mm. Male has a flattened, fat, pale blue body with yellow patches along each side. Brownish-yellow female and immature have yellow spots along each side, and look rather like giant wasps. Fast flier.

HABITAT Still or slow-flowing water at up to 1,200m. Distributed across Europe from Wales and England, and from southern Sweden south to Mediterranean.

FOOD AND HABITS Flies early May–early August. Feeds on insects. Tends to rest on waterside plants.

Common Darter
Sympetrum striolatum

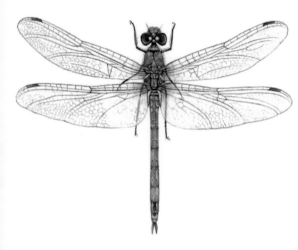

SIZE AND DESCRIPTION Length 35–44mm; hindwing 24–30mm. Mature male is red with a narrow pointed abdomen. Female and immatures are yellowish to light brown. Flies busily.

HABITAT Ponds, lakes, ditches and brackish waters at up to 1,800m. Distributed across Europe from Ireland, and south from southern Scandinavia to North Africa.

FOOD AND HABITS Flies June–October. Feeds on insects. Usually seen in large numbers. Often perches on twigs.

Ruddy Darter
Sympetrum sanguineum

SIZE AND DESCRIPTION Length 34–39mm; hindwing 23–51mm. Male is blood-red with a club-shaped rather than tapering abdomen. Yellow female has black thorax markings. Flitting and sometimes jerky flight.
HABITAT Shallow and well-vegetated (even brackish or acid) pools, ponds, lakes, ditches and canals at up to 1,000m. Distributed from Ireland across Europe, and south from southern Scandinavia. British population, which is strongest in south-east England, is supplemented by immigrants from the Continent in summer.
FOOD AND HABITS Flies June–October. Feeds on insects. Often perches.

Meadow Grasshopper
Chorthippus parallelus

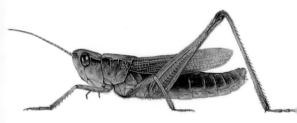

Size and description Length 13–16mm (m), 17–33mm (f). Grey, green, brown or purple in colour. Wings are short, reaching almost to the tip of male's abdomen; female's are even shorter, only half as long (this species cannot fly). Male's song comprises short, sewing-machine-like chirps in 1-second bursts, accomplished by rubbing small pegs on his legs across the veins on his forewings.

Habitat Meadows and grassland across northern Europe into Scandinavia, and mountain areas of Mediterranean. Absent from Ireland and the Isle of Man.

Food and habits Adults seen June–November. Feeds on leaves of grasses and sedges. Female lays eggs underground in the upper surface of soft soil, using her flexible ovipositor for digging and probing before egg laying.

Blue-winged Grasshopper
Oedipoda caerulescens

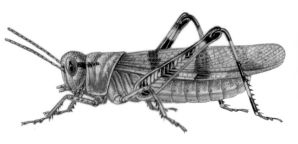

SIZE AND DESCRIPTION Length 17–26mm. Bright blue hindwings with a dark band near the outer edge. Mottled grey to almost black body and forewings, blending well with stony ground. No song.

HABITAT Warm, dry, stony and sandy areas in central and southern Europe. In Britain found only on Jersey and Guernsey.

FOOD AND HABITS Adults seen July–November. Coloured wings are used to confuse predators, who continue to look for the bright colour even when the grasshopper lands suddenly and closes its wings, 'changing' colour as it does so.

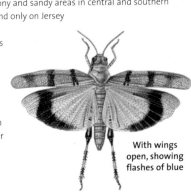

With wings open, showing flashes of blue

Common Field Grasshopper
Chorthippus brunneus

Size and description Length 14–18mm (m), 19–25mm (f). Colour green, purple or black. Wings are narrow and extend beyond the tip of the abdomen, and the underneath of the thorax is hairy. Male's abdomen has a reddish tip, which sometimes also occurs in female. Song is a hard 'sst' sound, repeated at 2-second intervals. Many grasshopper species have flexible abdomens which they use to dig a hole in soft soil and lay eggs.

Habitat Widespread in dry grassy areas, from Scandinavia to the Pyrenees and Italy. Particularly common in southern England.

Food and habits Adults seen July–October. Feeds mainly on grasses.

An egg-laying
female grasshopper

House Cricket
Acheta domesticus

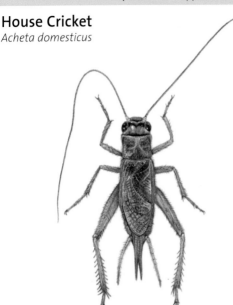

SIZE AND DESCRIPTION Length 16–20mm. Straw-coloured to brown body with black marks on the head. Wings extend beyond the tip of the abdomen. Female has a straight ovipositor that is up to 15mm long. Song a soft warble delivered at dusk or at night.

HABITAT A native insect of Asia and Africa, but now widespread in Europe. Usually lives in buildings, but may also be found in refuse tips in summer.

FOOD AND HABITS Feeds on refuse, but will also eat stored food.

Oak Bush-cricket
Meconema thalassinum

SIZE AND DESCRIPTION Length 12–15mm. Pale green with wings extending beyond the tip of the abdomen. Female has an upwards-curving ovipositor that extends well beyond her wings. Male has two thin, inwards-curving cerci, about 3mm long. Yellow or brownish stripe down the back, with two brown patches on either side. No song – male attracts female by drumming a hindleg against a leaf.

HABITAT Trees, particularly oaks, across Europe except Scotland, far north and far south.

FOOD AND HABITS Adults seen July–October. An insect-eating species that often comes to lights at night. Like all crickets and grasshoppers, has an 'incomplete' life cycle, without larval or pupal stages: on hatching it looks like a miniature of an adult, although its wings and sexual organs remain underdeveloped until it reaches maturity. The only tree-dwelling bush-cricket.

Life cycle of a cricket: from egg to adult

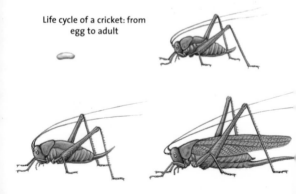

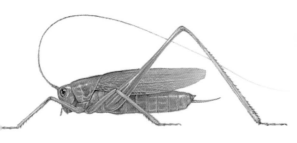

Oak tree,
a habitat

Speckled Bush-cricket
Leptophyes punctatissima

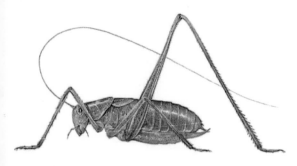

SIZE AND DESCRIPTION Length 10–14mm (m), 12–17mm (f). Yellow-green with fine red speckles. Very long and thin antennae. Narrow brown stripe along back, which may be very faint in female. Wings are short. Female has a long sickle-shaped ovipositor. Song is a sequence of soft 'zb' sounds at 3–6 second intervals.

HABITAT Gardens, parks and forest edges in undergrowth. Widespread from southern Scandinavia to Mediterranean, including Britain.

FOOD AND HABITS Adults seen July or August–October. Feeds on leaves, including those of Raspberry and rose bushes.

Common Earwig
Forficula auricularia

Length 10–15mm; pincers 4–9mm (m), 4–5mm (f). Long brown insect with an abdomen that is darker than the rest of its body. (White ones seen in gardens are in the process of moulting.) Pincers at the end of the body, with male's being more curved than female's. Abundant in Europe in many habitats. Very common in gardens. Mainly vegetarian. Female displays parental care, laying 20–50 eggs in soil and caring for them in winter; after the young hatch she feeds them until they are fully developed.

Small Earwig
Labia minor

Length 5mm; pincers to 2.5mm. Dull darkish-brown body and blackish head. Hindwings extend beyond forewings when at rest. Found in decaying vegetation. Common around compost heaps. Flies well, mostly at dusk. Breeds in manure heaps, and displays parental care for young.

German Cockroach
Blatta germanica

SIZE AND DESCRIPTION Length 10–13mm. Pale reddish-brown. The long wings extend beyond the tip of the abdomen. There are two longitudinal dark marks on the pronotum (the shield covering the head). It can fly, but rarely does so.

HABITAT Buildings, and rubbish tips in summer. Introduced from North Africa.

FOOD AND HABITS Scavenges for food on the ground.

Common Cockroach
Blatta orientalis

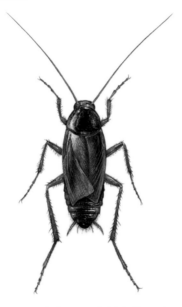

Size and description Length 18–30mm. Male's leathery wings extend to the last three segments of the abdomen; female's wings barely cover the thorax.

Habitat Warm indoors places; rubbish tips in summer. Survives outdoors in mild parts of Europe. Originated in Asia and Africa.

Food and habits Scavenges on the ground for food scraps and decaying matter.

Praying Mantis
Mantis religiosa

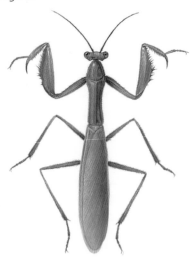

SIZE AND DESCRIPTION Length 50–60mm. Large green or brown insect with a triangular head, long wings and long legs. Males are particularly slender. The well-separated eyes enable it to track passing insects.

HABITAT Rough grassland, scrub and *maquis* in continental Europe, as far south as southern France. Not found in Britain.

FOOD AND HABITS Preys on other insects. Adopts a threat display, raising its neck and front legs in a 'praying' posture. Uses its spiky front legs to spear insect prey very fast. Female eats male after or during copulation.

Booklouse *Liposcelis terricolis*

Length 1–2mm. Brown and flat-bodied with a large head. There are several similar species. Occurs indoors, and is commonly found among old books. Feeds on books, paper and stored food.

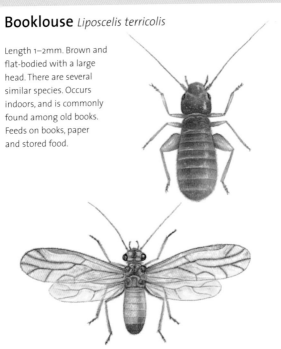

Bark Louse *Caecilius flavidus*

Length 1–2mm. Body is yellow, and wings are bristly. Lives in broadleaved trees. Very common throughout Europe. Feeds on algae and pollen on foliage of trees. Males are unknown. Females reproduce by parthenogenesis (a type of nonsexual reproduction in which an organism develops from an unfertilized ovum).

Forest Bug
Pentatoma rufipes

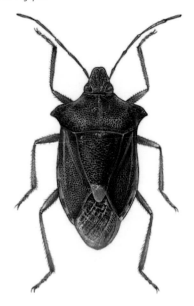

SIZE AND DESCRIPTION Length 12–15mm. Dark brown with a thorax that protrudes like a yoke. Reddish legs.

HABITAT Found on trees (in particular cherry trees) in orchards and shrubberies.

FOOD AND HABITS Adults seen June–October. An omnivorous bug that sucks juice from buds, leaves and fruits, and attacks other insects.

Hawthorn Shield Bug
Acanthosoma haemorrhoidale

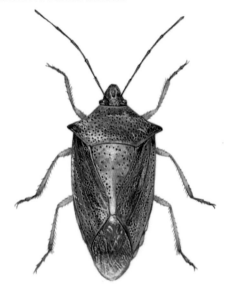

SIZE AND DESCRIPTION Length 15mm. Body is shield-shaped with a reddish-brown band along the rear of the thorax.

HABITAT Woodland edges, hedgerows and gardens with hedges and shrubs. Widespread in Europe, but absent from Scotland.

FOOD AND HABITS Eats the leaves of hawthorn and fruit trees. Basks on walls in autumn before hibernating.

Green Shield Bug
Palomena prasina

SIZE AND DESCRIPTION Length 10–15mm. Bright green in spring and summer, bronze-coloured in autumn. Wing-tips are dark brown. Larvae resemble small wingless adults. Shield bugs derive their name from their scutellum – a large triangular plate that covers the front of the abdomen and reaches the tip of the folded wing membrane.
HABITAT Woodland edges and glades, hedgerows, and gardens with shrubs and herbaceous borders over much of Europe.
FOOD AND HABITS Eats the leaves of trees such as hazels and oaks, shrubs and herbaceous plants. Hibernates in leaf litter.

Common
Hazel, a
foodplant

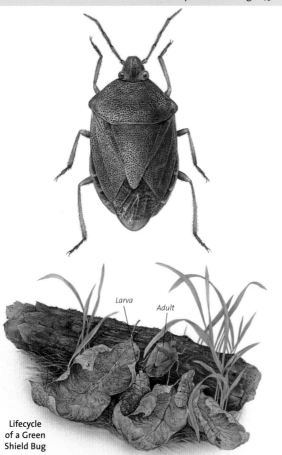

Larva　*Adult*

Lifecycle of a Green Shield Bug

Black-kneed Capsid
Blepharidopterus angulatus

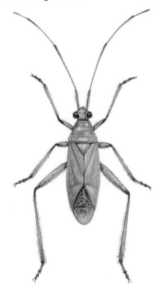

Size and description Length 15mm. Green with a narrower body than that of Common Green Capsid (page 54). Legs have black patches on the 'knees'.

Habitat Orchard trees, particularly apples and limes.

Food and habits A predatory insect that is beneficial to orchard owners because it feeds on Red Spider Mites, which cause damage to fruit trees. Makes a 'squeak' by rubbing the tip of its beak against its thorax. Will stab with its beak if handled.

Fire Bug
Pyrrhocoris apterus

SIZE AND DESCRIPTION Length 10mm. Red and black with black spots on
the red forewings.

HABITAT Found in open country in central and southern Europe. Rare
in Britain, occurring only in the far south of England.

FOOD AND HABITS Omnivorous, feeding on fallen seeds and preying
upon other insects. Adults hibernate.

Hot-bed Bug
Xylocoris galactinus

Length 6mm. Brownish wings with translucent tips. Through a lens, it is possible to see that the antennae are hairy. Found in compost heaps, hot-beds and other areas with warm soil. Also occurs in birds' nests and stables. Feeds on other insects, and will suck the blood of birds.

Common Flower Bug
Anthocoris nemorum

Length 3–4mm. Shiny and generally brownish, with a black spot on greyish forewings. Head is black. Found on almost any type of tree, shrub or herbaceous plant. Occurs over most of Europe. A predator of aphids, Red Spider Mites and other insects. Adults hibernate under loose bark and in clumps of grass.

Fly Bug
Reduvius personatus

Length 17mm. Dark brown to black. Bristly legs and abdomen. Wings extend to the tip of the abdomen. Found in places with plenty of crevices; most common around human habitation. Occurs in much of Europe, including southern England. A nocturnal feeder on small insects, including bed bugs. Makes a 'squeak' by rubbing the tip of its beak against its thorax. Will stab with its beak if handled.

Tarnished Plant Bug
Lygus rugulipennis

Length 4–6mm. Variable colour, from yellow to red or brown. Wing-tips are membranous. Rather bristly legs. Occurs in gardens and other places with plenty of vegetation, over most of Europe. Feeds on potatoes and other crops, as well as flowers and nettles. Causes white spots on leaves. Winters in leaf litter. Most common in late summer.

Common Green Capsid
Lygocoris pabulinus

Raspberries, a food plant

SIZE AND DESCRIPTION Length 5–7mm. Green with greyish wing-tips and bristly legs. Potato Capsid is similar, but has two black spots behind its head.

HABITAT Found in most of Europe, wherever there is plentiful vegetation.

FOOD AND HABITS Flies May–October. Eggs laid on woody plants hatch in spring. Eats herbaceous plants, potatoes and soft fruits such as raspberries and gooseberries.

Water Measurer
Hydrometra stagnorum

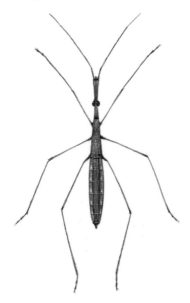

SIZE AND DESCRIPTION Length 11mm. Narrow body, greatly elongated head and long legs. Usually wingless.

HABITAT Found on the surface of still or slow-flowing water throughout much of Europe.

FOOD AND HABITS Feeds on water fleas, insect larvae and other small animals, which it spears from the surface with its beak. Moves slowly across the water's surface.

Common Pond Skater
Gerris lacustris

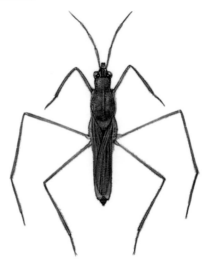

Size and description Length 10mm. Has a broader body than Water Measurer (page 55) and a considerably shorter head, which has largish eyes. Usually fully winged. There are several similar species. 'Skates' over the surface of the water.

Habitat Ponds, lakes and slow-running rivers throughout Europe.

Food and habits Senses vibrations made by other insects. When swimming, moves across the water's surface with a rowing action of the middle legs. The hindlegs act as rudders, while the front legs catch insects that fall into the water. Flies away from water in order to hibernate.

Water Scorpion
Nepa cinerea

Size and description Length 20mm; tail 8mm. Flattened brown body equipped with strong scorpion-like front legs and a snorkel at the rear. Fully winged, but rarely flies.

Habitat Shallow still water and pond margins. Occurs across Europe.

Food and habits Walks slowly over plants or mud just under the water. Breathes through its hollow snorkel-like 'tail', which draws in air as it protrudes above the surface. Active throughout the year, feeding on invertebrates and small fish, which are caught with its powerful front legs.

Water Stick Insect
Ranatra linearis

SIZE AND DESCRIPTION Length 50mm. Huge pincers and a long air tube at the hind end like that of Water Scorpion (page 57), to which it is closely related. The breathing tube is stuck out through the surface of the water to breathe air.

HABITAT Inhabits weedy still-water ponds and lakes. Widely distributed throughout Europe except far north and south. Fairly common in southern England and Wales.

FOOD AND HABITS Adopts a mantid-like posture when submerged and ambushes passing aquatic creatures, catching them with its front legs. Looks rather like a twig, and this camouflage helps it to creep up on its prey.

Common Backswimmer
Notonecta glauca

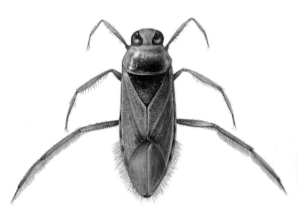

SIZE AND DESCRIPTION Length 16mm. Long and bristly hindlegs. Swims on its back, which is keeled, clutching a large air-bubble to its underside and 'rowing' with its back legs. One of several species of water boatman. Also called Great Water Boatman.

HABITAT Common in ponds, lakes and slow-running rivers across Britain and continental Europe.

FOOD AND HABITS A fierce hunter of tadpoles, small fish and other insects. Active all year round. Will fly in warm weather.

Swims on its back

Punctate Corixa
Corixa punctata

Size and description Length 12–14mm. Triangular head lacks a rostrum. Swims with its back upwards, unlike the similar-looking Common Backswimmer (page 59). Courting male sings loudly by rubbing the hair patches on the insides of his front legs against his head. One of 15 species of lesser water boatman.

Habitat Widespread in still waters. Occurs throughout Europe except far north and uplands.

Food and habits Feeds on plant debris and microscopic organisms. Capable of flight.

Cicada
Cicadetta montana

SIZE AND DESCRIPTION Length 18mm. Long, transparent and shiny wings. Dark pronotum. Three spines on the front femur. Male produces a soft warble by vibrating small membranes on the sides of his body.

HABITAT Woodland clearings and scrubby areas in central and southern Europe. In Britain found only in the New Forest.

FOOD AND HABITS Flies May–August. Feeds on pines and other trees, sucking their sap with its sturdy beak.

Potato Leafhopper
Eupteryx aurata

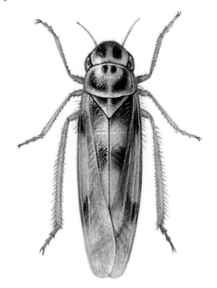

SIZE AND DESCRIPTION Length 4mm. Black-and-yellow pattern that is often orange-tinged. Wings reach past the tip of the abdomen.
HABITAT Wasteland, gardens and hedgerows throughout Europe except far north.
FOOD AND HABITS Adults seen May–December. Sucks sap from herbaceous plants.

Common Froghopper
Philaenus spumarius

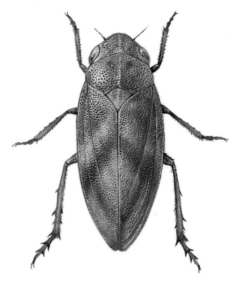

SIZE AND DESCRIPTION Length 6mm. Variable brown pattern. Wings held together like a tent. Young coat themselves in a white froth called 'cuckoo-spit' – the sap of a plant that has passed through them – which acts as a protection from predators and from drying out. Adults do look a little like frogs from above, and jump well.

HABITAT Woody and herbaceous plants. Found throughout Europe except far north.

FOOD AND HABITS Flies June–September. Feeds on plant sap.

Rose Aphid
Macrosiphum rosae

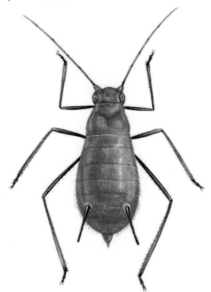

SIZE AND DESCRIPTION Length 1–2mm. Green or pink greenfly. Long black cornicles on the abdomen, which are not found on other aphids.
HABITAT Woodland edges, hedges and gardens throughout Europe.
FOOD AND HABITS Feeds on roses in spring, and scabious or teasel in summer.

Black Bean Aphid
Aphis fabae

Length 2mm. Black or olive
in colour. May be wingless.
Occurs across Europe where
there are suitable food plants.
Feeds on the young shoots of
dock, beans, spinach, beet,
nasturtium and other plants.
Eggs are laid on shrubs such
as Spindle and philadelphius.

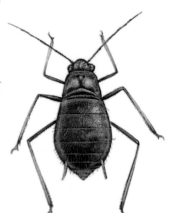

Cabbage Whitefly
Ateryrodes protella

Length 2–3mm. Waxy-white
wings. Found in fields and
gardens all over Europe, on
the undersides of cabbage
leaves. Sucks the sap from
cabbage leaves. Active
throughout the year.

Woolly Aphid
Eriosoma langerum

SIZE AND DESCRIPTION Length 1–2mm. Purplish-brown with or without wings, and covered with strands of whitish fluffy wax.

HABITAT Orchards and gardens across Europe. Accidentally introduced from America.

FOOD AND HABITS Sucks the sap of fruit trees. Most young are born live by parthogenesis (an aesexual form of reproduction in which an unfertilized egg develops into a new individual).

Cabbage Aphid
Aleyrodes proletella

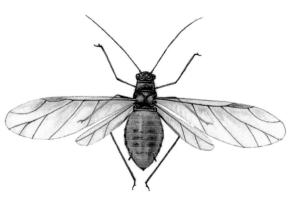

SIZE AND DESCRIPTION Length 2mm. Winged individuals are dark green and black. Wingless individuals have a mealy-white covering.
HABITAT Wasteland and farmland throughout Europe. Abundant in spring and summer.
FOOD AND HABITS Feeds on brassicas in spring and early summer.

Thunder-fly
Aeolothrips intermedius

Length 2.5mm. Blackish body with brown-barred wings. Inhabits well-vegetated open areas. Eats the sap of yellow crucifers and compositae.

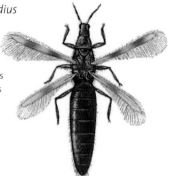

Pea Thrips
Kakothrips pisivorus

Length 2.5mm. Black body with white feathery wings. Inhabits well-vegetated open areas, gardens and allotments. Scrapes pea-pods to reach their sap, leaving silvery patches on pods where it has been feeding.

Green Lacewing

Chrysopa pallens

SIZE AND DESCRIPTION Length 15–20mm; wingspan 30–40mm. Bright
green body, golden eyes and green veins on transparent wings. There
are several species of lacewing in continental Europe, and two similar
species in Britain.

HABITAT Woods, hedgerows, gardens and well-vegetated areas. Found
in most of Europe, but not Scotland and northern Scandinavia.

FOOD AND HABITS Flies May–August. Mainly nocturnal. Adults and larvae
prey on aphids.

Furniture Beetle
Anobium punctatum

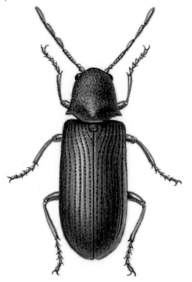

SIZE AND DESCRIPTION Length 2.5–5mm. Colour of elytra, which are ridged, varies from dark brown to yellowish. Antennae are clubbed. Covered with fine down.

HABITAT Dry wood of deciduous and coniferous trees. Abundant in houses. Found across central and northern Europe.

FOOD AND HABITS Seen May–July. Larvae are woodworm. Their presence is shown only by the escape holes of the emerging adults, which are 1.5–2mm in diameter.

Larder Beetle
Dermestes lardarius

SIZE AND DESCRIPTION Length 7–9.5mm. An oval-shaped beetle. Pale markings on elytra may be greenish, greyish or brownish. Larva is short and covered in hairs.

HABITAT Houses and also birds' nests. Occurs throughout central and northern Europe.

FOOD AND HABITS Found all year round, with both larvae and adults feeding on carrion and dried meats in store. In houses larvae feed on animal products.

Carabid Beetle
Carabus nemoralis

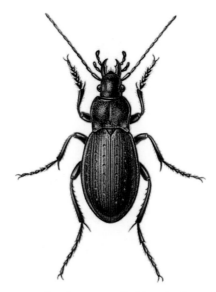

SIZE AND DESCRIPTION Length 20–30mm. Black tinged with metallic colours varying from bronze to brassy green. Elytra are pitted in lines and finely ridged. Female is less shiny than male.

HABITAT Most habitats across Europe, but not northern Scandinavia.

FOOD AND HABITS Fast-moving flightless beetle that is a nocturnal predator of ground-dwelling invertebrates.

Violet Ground Beetle
Carabus violaceus

SIZE AND DESCRIPTION Length 20–35mm. Black with violet tinges to the thorax and elytra. Thorax is flanged and the elytra have a smooth oval shape. Larva has a shiny black head and thorax, and a long, segmented dusky body.
HABITAT Woods, hedges, gardens and scrub.
FOOD AND HABITS Non-flying, fast-running nocturnal predator of invertebrates. Larva is also a predator, but is less agile than the adult beetle.

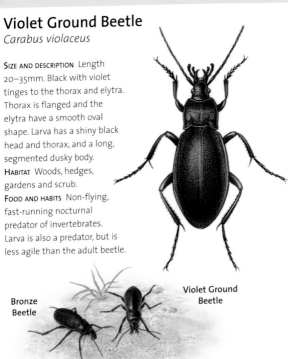

Bronze Beetle

Violet Ground Beetle

▲ SIMILAR SPECIES **Bronze Beetle** *C. granulatus* 16–23mm long. The most common Irish ground beetle, but local in the UK. Ubiquitous in wet fields, river margins, fens, lake shores and upland peat; occasionally found in gardens. Widespread in continental Europe and Siberia to the Pacific coast.

Churchyard Beetle
Blaps mucronata

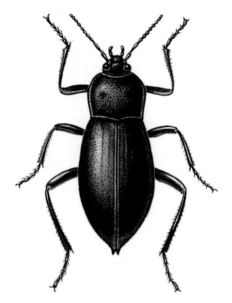

SIZE AND DESCRIPTION Length 18mm. Entirely black with pitted elytra that taper at the ends to form a pointed tip.

HABITAT Dark places such as caves, cellars and stables throughout northern and central Europe.

FOOD AND HABITS Flightless nocturnal scavenger on vegetable matter. Emits a foul smell when threatened.

Minotaur Beetle
Typhaeus typhoeus

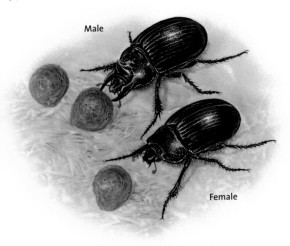

Male

Female

SIZE AND DESCRIPTION Length 12–20mm. Entirely black with shiny ribbed elytra. Male has three pointed horns on the pronotum, the middle one being the shortest. Female has just two short points.

HABITAT Heathland and dry sandy grassland. Occurs throughout Europe except far north.

FOOD AND HABITS Seen year round, but most common in spring and autumn. Often flies during the evening. Buries mainly rabbit dung in burrows up to 1m deep, in which larvae develop. Like all dung beetles, it gets rid of dung in a useful way, burying it and helping in the recycling of soil nutrients.

Dor Beetle
Geotrupes stercorarius

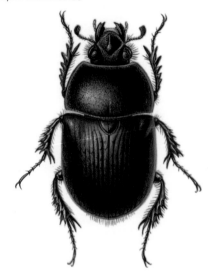

SIZE AND DESCRIPTION Length 16–25mm. Broad rounded dung beetle that is shiny green or blue underneath. Each elytra has seven ridges, and the legs are thick and hairy. Also called Lousy Watchman due to the large number of mites on it.

HABITAT Range of habitats including gardens. Occurs throughout Britain and much of continental Europe.

FOOD AND HABITS Seen April–October. Digs burrows under dung. Takes dung to a chamber at the end of a burrow, where eggs are laid and larvae feed on the dung. Flies well on warm evenings.

Horned Dung Beetle
Copris lunaris

Dor Beetle (also
opposite)

Horned
Dung Beetle

SIZE AND DESCRIPTION Length 15–25mm. Very shiny, stoutly built black
dung beetle with ribbed elytra. Male has a slender horn on the head;
female's horn is much shorter. Also called English Scarab.

HABITAT Grassland such as grazing pastures. Found throughout Europe
except far north. Rare in Britain; found only in southern England.

FOOD AND HABITS Dormant in winter. Breeds mainly in cow dung, which
is scraped up with the head and legs, shaped into a ball, and rolled
along with the hindlegs to deep shafts excavated under cowpats,
where adult female beetles feed and lay their eggs. Flies well.

Green Tiger Beetle
Cicindela campestris

SIZE AND DESCRIPTION Length 10–15mm. Green with pale spots on the elytra. Some individuals are darker than others, and the markings may be variable. Long and shiny legs, powerful jaws and large eyes.
HABITAT Sandy areas such as heaths and sand dunes. Found throughout Britain and in much of continental Europe.
FOOD AND HABITS Seen April–September. Feeds on insects, which it chases on the ground. Able to run fast – one of the fastest running insects there is. Larvae lurk in burrows and ambush passing prey. Flies with a buzzing sound when disturbed.

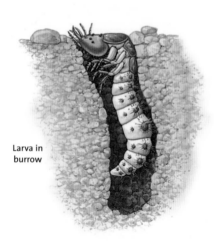

Larva in
burrow

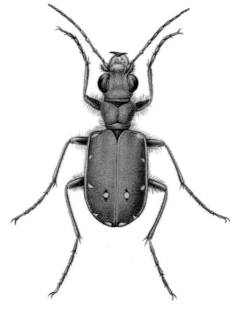

Front view
of adult

Rove beetle
Oxytelus laquaetus

SIZE AND DESCRIPTION
Length 6mm. Rove
beetle with small.
brown elytra and
yellowish legs.
HABITAT Compost
heaps in gardens.
FOOD AND HABITS Feeds
on rotting vegetable
material and the grubs
of other insects found
in manure heaps.
Flies well.

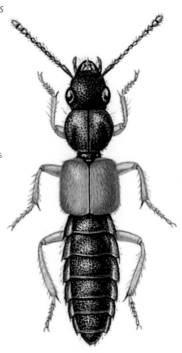

Devil's Coach Horse
Staphylinus olens

SIZE AND DESCRIPTION Length
20–30mm. Black with
small and almost square
elytra, which leave the
long abdomen exposed.
HABITAT Woods, hedges,
parks and gardens
throughout Europe. Often
found in damp outhouses.
FOOD AND HABITS Nocturnal
predator with powerful
jaws. Feeds on slugs and
other invertebrates. When
under threat, raises its tail
and opens its jaws.

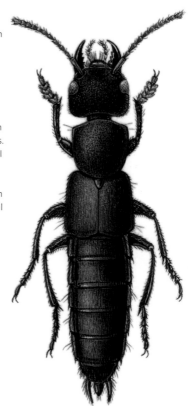

Black Beetle
Feronia nigrita

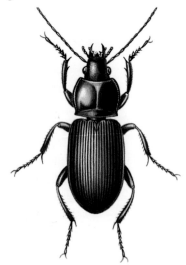

SIZE AND DESCRIPTION Length 16mm. Jet black with ridges running down the elytra.
HABITAT Woods, gardens and parks throughout Europe.
FOOD AND HABITS Nocturnal predator of other invertebrates.

Lesser Stag Beetle
Dorcas parallelipipedus

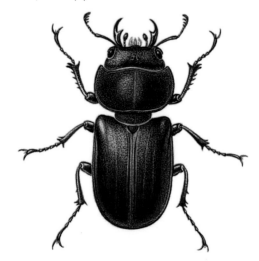

SIZE AND DESCRIPTION Length 19–32mm. Large grey-black beetle rather like a considerably smaller female Stag Beetle (page 84). Male has larger jaws than female, but a great deal smaller than those of a male Stag Beetle, and similar to female's of that species. Male also has a particularly wide head.

HABITAT Deciduous woods, parks and gardens with large trees and orchards. Widespread throughout northern and central Europe.

FOOD AND HABITS Flies April–October. Adults may be seen flying at dusk. Feeds on sap. C-shaped larvae live in soft decaying wood, especially that of ashes, beeches and apples.

Stag Beetle
Lucanus cervinus

SIZE AND DESCRIPTION Length 25–75mm. The biggest beetle in Europe.
Smooth chestnut to almost black, with a black head and thorax.
Male's huge jaws look like antlers (hence the beetle's name). Female
has normal jaws, and is smaller than male. Brown-headed whitish
larva is about 75mm long when fully grown.

HABITAT Oakwoods, parks and gardens with old trees across central
and southern Europe. Scarce in Britain, but may be seen in the south,
notably the Greater London area. In serious decline everywhere, so
British population is of conservation importance.

FOOD AND HABITS Flies May–August during evenings and at night. Feeds
on tree sap. Breeding males wrestle with their 'antlers'. Larvae eat
decaying wood, living in the stumps and roots of oaks and elms. They
take 3–5 years to reach maturity, but adults live for only a few weeks.

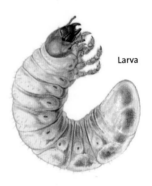

Larva

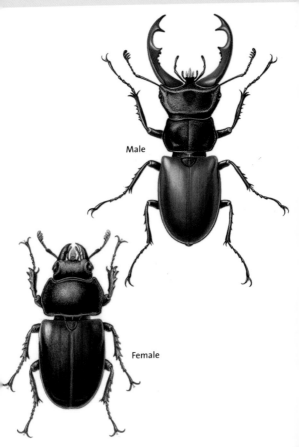

Male

Female

Rose Chafer
Cetonia aurata

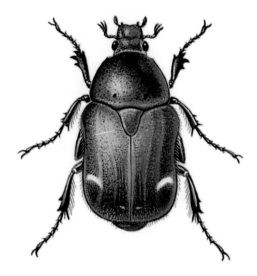

SIZE AND DESCRIPTION Length 14–18mm. Flattened squarish elytra are usually green, but may be bronze or bluish-black.

HABITAT Woodland margins, hedges, scrub and gardens in southern and central Europe, including southern England.

FOOD AND HABITS Adults fly May–August by day, and nibble petals and stamens of flowers. Larvae feed in decaying wood and take 2–3 years to develop.

Cockchafer
Melolontha melolontha

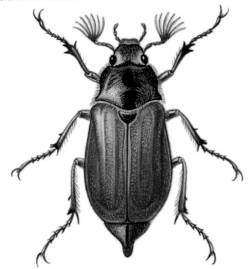

SIZE AND DESCRIPTION Length 20–30mm. Black thorax. Rusty elytra do
not quite cover abdomen, exposing the pointed tip. Legs are brown
and antennae fan out. Male has larger antennae than female. Whitish
larva has a brown head, but is smaller and more wrinkly than a Stag
Beetle larva (page 84). Also called Maybug.

HABITAT Woodland margins, parks and gardens. Common throughout
Europe, but absent above 1,000m and from far north.

FOOD AND HABITS Flies May–July at night. Adults chew the leaves of
trees and shrubs. Larvae feed on roots and take three years to develop.

Summer Chafer
Amphimallon solstitialis

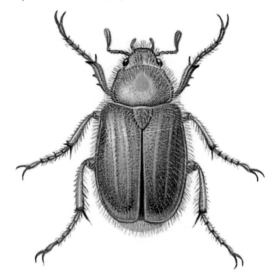

SIZE AND DESCRIPTION Length 14–18mm. Entirely brown and hairy. Antennae have only three flaps to them.

HABITAT Parks, gardens, scrub and hedges throughout most of Europe.

FOOD AND HABITS Adults swarm around deciduous trees and bushes at dusk and at night. Will fly to lighted windows. Larvae feed on grass roots and take up to two years to mature.

Garden Chafer
Phyllopertha horticola

SIZE AND DESCRIPTION Length 8.5–11mm. Dark metallic green or black head and thorax, and brown elytra, sometimes with iridescence.
HABITAT Rough grassland, orchards and gardens with large lawns throughout Europe except far north.
FOOD AND HABITS Flies June–July, usually by day. Adults chew the leaves of trees and shrubs. Larvae, which take 2–3 years to develop, feed on grass roots.

Lined Click Beetle
Agriotes lineatus

SIZE AND DESCRIPTION Length
7.5–10mm. Bullet-shaped
with lined elytra. Thorax
is either black or brown.
HABITAT Grassland and
cultivated land in central
and northern Europe.
FOOD AND HABITS Can
be seen most of the
year, but most common
in May–August. Larvae,
which are commonly
known as 'wireworms',
can be a serious pest
of cultivated plants.

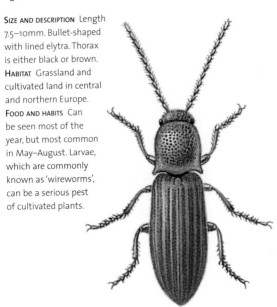

Click beetle
Athous haemorrhoidalis

SIZE AND DESCRIPTION Length
7–10mm. Long black or dark
brown thorax and ridged brown
back. Larva is brown with a thin
segmented body.
HABITAT Grassland, including
parks and gardens, throughout
Europe except far north.
FOOD AND HABITS Flies May–July.
Adults chew grasses and
flowers, especially stamens with
pollen. Larvae cause severe
damage to roots. Click beetles
are so-called because they
can flip over when threatened
or overturned, propelling
themselves up to 30cm into
the air. They do this by bending
their body, making an audible
click as they do so.

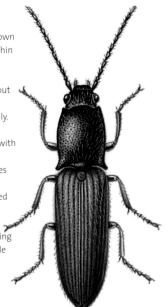

Soldier beetle
Cantharis rustica

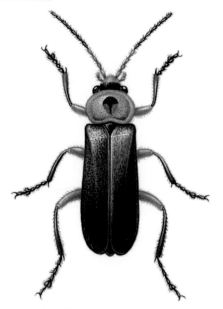

SIZE AND DESCRIPTION Length 11–14mm. Black elytra. Orange thorax
bears a dark mark. Antennae are beaded. Larva has a flattened and
segmented dark brown body.

HABITAT Abundant in damp situations, including woodland edges
and open country, throughout Europe.

FOOD AND HABITS Flies May–August. Preys on other insects, located
on flower blossoms.

Cardinal Beetle
Pyrochroa coccinea

SIZE AND DESCRIPTION Length 14–18mm. Bright reddish-orange elytra and thorax, with a black head and feathery antennae. Legs are black. Larvae are yellowish-brown with a squarish rear end.

HABITAT Woodland edges in northern and central Europe.

FOOD AND HABITS Flies May–July. Found on flowers and old tree trunks. Larvae live under bark and prey on other insects.

Two-spot Ladybird
Adalia bipunctata

SIZE AND DESCRIPTION Length 3.5–5.5mm. Varies greatly, with northern populations often being largely black. Most common form is red with a bold black spot on each elytron. Larva is similar to that of Seven-spot Ladybird (page 96). One of 46 ladybird species in Britain.
HABITAT Well-vegetated habitats throughout Europe. Abundant.
FOOD AND HABITS Flies spring–autumn, eating aphids on herbaceous and woody plants. Winters in groups (sometimes containing as many as 1,000 individuals) in sheds and houses. Sites are used by successive generations.

Twenty-two-spot Ladybird
Thea 22-punctata

SIZE AND DESCRIPTION Length 5mm. Lemon yellow with 10 or 11 black spots on each elytron and 5 spots on the pronotum.

HABITAT Well-vegetated places throughout Europe.

FOOD AND HABITS Flies April–August. Eats mildew on umbellifers and other plants. Winters in leaf litter, but may appear in mild weather.

Seven-spot Ladybird
Coccinella 7-punctata

SIZE AND DESCRIPTION Length 5.2–8mm. Bright-red elytra with seven black spots, although some individuals may have more or fewer spots. Thorax is black with patches of pale yellow at the front corners. Larva is steely blue with yellow or cream spots.

HABITAT Well-vegetated habitats, including gardens, throughout central and northern Europe. Common and widespread in Britain.

FOOD AND HABITS Flies early spring–autumn. Both adults and larvae feed on aphids. Eggs are laid in small groups on leaves. When threatened, adults exude a distasteful bright yellow substance from the leg joints as a deterrent to potential predators. Adults overwinter in garden sheds, vegetation, crevices in fences and similar locations, frequently in relatively large numbers.

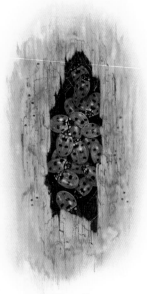

Hibernating ladybirds

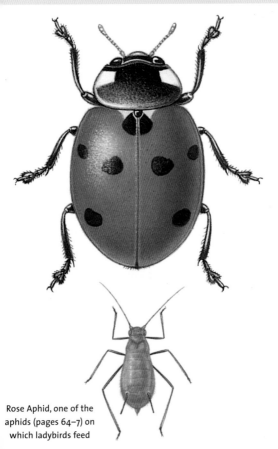

Rose Aphid, one of the
aphids (pages 64–7) on
which ladybirds feed

Harlequin Ladybird
Harmonia axyridis

SIZE AND DESCRIPTION Length
7–9mm. Highly variable,
with elytra ground colour
ranging from pale yellow-
orange to red or black.
Most common forms in
Britain are orange with
15–21 black spots, and
black with 2 or 4 orange
or red spots.

HABITAT Very diverse
habitats, but most
common on deciduous
trees and low-growing
plants such as nettles.
Invasive Asian species
introduced to North
America in 1988; invaded
much of north-west
Europe, arriving in Britain
in 2004. There are fears
that it will out-compete
native species.

FOOD AND HABITS Feeds
most commonly on
aphids, but also many
other small insects,
including other ladybirds,
and pollen.

Dark morph

Light morph

False Ladybird
Endomychus coccineus

SIZE AND DESCRIPTION Length 4–6mm. Red with four large black spots. Less rotund than a ladybird. Larva is brightly coloured.

HABITAT Woodland, especially beechwoods.

FOOD AND HABITS Flies April–June. Eats fungus and lives under the bark of dying or dead trees. The larvae crawl around openly on wood fungi.

Raspberry Beetle
Byturus tomentosus

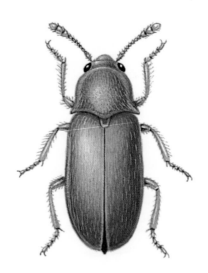

SIZE AND DESCRIPTION Length 3.2–4mm. Yellowish-brown or greyish, and hairy.

HABITAT Open areas with scrub and bushes, including gardens. Occurs throughout central and northern Europe.

FOOD AND HABITS Adults, which are present May–July, gnaw flower buds. Larvae develop in blackberries and raspberries, feeding on the developing fruits.

Wasp Beetle
Clytus arictis

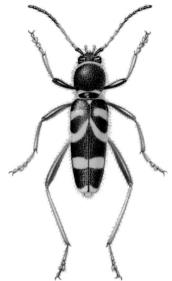

SIZE AND DESCRIPTION Length 7–14mm. Long-legged black longhorn beetle with very variable yellow bands on the elytra.

HABITAT Woods, gardens, parks and hedges throughout Europe except far north. Common in most of Britain and may often be seen in gardens in the south; less frequent and more local in the north.

FOOD AND HABITS Seen May–July, often feeding on flower nectar and pollen. Female lays eggs in dead wood, and larvae feed on the wood for at least two years. A harmless wasp mimic.

Potato Flea Beetle
Psylliodes affinis

SIZE AND DESCRIPTION Length 2.8mm. Reddish-brown beetle with thick black thighs on the hind legs.

HABITAT Common on nightshades and potatoes in Europe, including southern and central Britain.

FOOD AND HABITS Adults nibble leaves, while larvae feed on roots. Beetles hibernate under bark and leaf litter, emerging in spring to resume feeding.

Musk Beetle
Aromia moschata

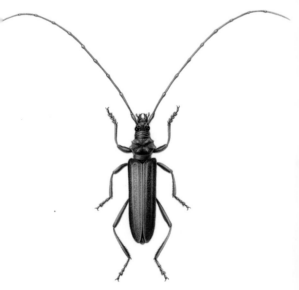

Size and description Length 13–34mm. Striking metallic green or blue beetle. Antennae are as long as, or longer than, the combined head and body length.

Habitat Deciduous woodland, especially willow, across central Europe. Local in southern Britain.

Food and habits Flies June–August. Emits a musky secretion. Larvae develop in willows, particularly old pollards.

Pea Weevil
Sitona lineatus

Size and description Length 4–5mm. Pale and dark brown stripes run along the body. Eyes are very prominent.

Habitat Found wherever wild and cultivated leguminous plants grow. Native to Europe, but absent from northern Scandinavia.

Food and habits Adults, which are mainly active in spring and autumn, chew semi-circular pieces from the edges of leaves and may damage seedlings. Larvae live inside root nodules. There are several species of weevil that attack garden plants.

Nut Weevil
Curculio nucum

SIZE AND DESCRIPTION Length 6–9mm, including the 'snout', or rostrum, which is longer in female than in male. Feathery antennae stem from the rostrum.

HABITAT Woods, parks and gardens with oaks and hazels. Found in central and northern Europe.

FOOD AND HABITS Adults seen April–July visiting hawthorn blossom for nectar. Female uses her long snout to drill into a young hazelnut, then lays an egg in the hole. The emerging larva feeds on the kernel until autumn, when the nut falls to the ground. The larva gnaws its way out of the nut and digs into the soil to pupate over winter.

Oak Weevil
Curculio villosus

SIZE AND DESCRIPTION Length 4–5mm, including rostrum. Patchy grey and black.
HABITAT Woods, parks and gardens with oaks throughout Europe except far north.
FOOD AND HABITS Found in oak trees in summer. Female uses her long snout to bore into acorns, laying her eggs in them. Larvae develop within the acorns.

Hawthorn Fruit Weevil
Rhynchites aequatus

SIZE AND DESCRIPTION Length 2.5–4.5mm. Slightly hairy elytra are yellow, red or brown. Also called Apple Fruit Weevil.

HABITAT Hawthorn, apple and other fruit trees in southern Britain and most of continental Europe.

FOOD AND HABITS Seen spring–autumn. Has a two-year life cycle. Female bores into apples or haws with her snout, then lays eggs in them; she chews the stems and the fruits shrivel. Larvae stay in fruits until autumn, then leave and cover themselves with soil. Adults emerge from the pupae about a year later, but stay underground until spring.

Whirligig beetle
Gyrinus natator

SIZE AND DESCRIPTION Length
6–7mm. Tiny shiny black beetle
that gyrates on the water's
surface and dives rapidly when
alarmed. Middle and hind legs are
short and oar-like. Two-part eyes
enable it to look down into the
water and across the surface
simultaneously.

HABITAT Occurs in both still and
slow-moving water. There are
several species of whirligig beetle
in Europe.

FOOD AND HABITS Visible for much
of the year, but hibernates. Preys
on mosquito larvae and insects
that fall into the water. Dives
rapidly down into the water when
disturbed. Often seen in small
groups. Lays eggs on submerged
plants. Larvae stay on the bottom
until they are nearly fully grown.

Great Diving Beetle
Dytiscus marginalis

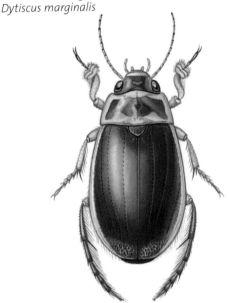

Size and description Length 27–35mm. Dark brown to black, fringed with yellowish-brown. Females have ridged elytra, while males have smooth ones. Larva has well-developed legs and a segmented body that bends more than that of a dragonfly nymph.

Habitat Prefers reedy ponds and other still waters. The most common European diving beetle.

Food and habits Flies at night. Prey includes newts, tadpoles, small fish and insects. Larvae live underwater and are voracious predators.

Diving beetle
Colymbetes fuscus

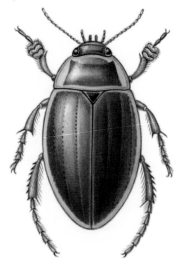

SIZE AND DESCRIPTION Length 17–19mm. Rather like a small Great Diving Beetle (page 109), but smoother and more uniformly oval in shape. Often has a green iridescence.

HABITAT Stagnant weedy ponds and ditches throughout central and northern Europe.

FOOD AND HABITS Can be found during most of the year, although it may hibernate during the coldest winter months. A predator of other invertebrates.

Diving beetle
Hydroporus palustris

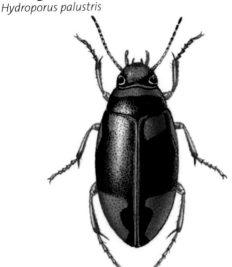

SIZE AND DESCRIPTION Length 3–3.3mm. Oval-shaped elytra. Black with patches of orange or yellowish-brown. One of 34 species in a genus of diving water beetles found in Europe.

HABITAT Common in all types of still water throughout central and northern Europe.

FOOD AND HABITS Flies at night. Preys on a variety of small aquatic invertebrates. Comes to the surface for air, which it carries in a bubble beneath its elytra when it dives.

Water scavenger beetle
Hydrobius fuscipes

SIZE AND DESCRIPTION Length 6mm. Black with a metallic sheen. Can be distinguished by the pitted furrows along the elytra. Legs are rust coloured. Very flat underside. Larva is maggot-like.

HABITAT Still waters throughout Europe.

FOOD AND HABITS Omnivorous scavenger that does not swim well and crawls over underwater plants. Collects air from the surface by swimming to it head first and storing air beneath its elytra. Larvae are predatory on other aquatic invertebrates.

Cat Flea
Ctenocephalides felis

SIZE AND DESCRIPTION Length
2.5mm. Male is slightly
smaller than female.
HABITAT Found mostly in
houses containing cats
and dogs. Breeds rapidly
in warm weather.
FOOD AND HABITS Most
abundant in summer.
A blood-sucker. Can jump
vertically for about 15cm.
Will bite humans and
other mammals.

Human Flea
Pules irritans

SIZE AND DESCRIPTION 3.5mm.
Very similar to Cat Flea.
HABITAT Found in buildings,
and on humans, badgers
and foxes.
FOOD AND HABITS Feeds on
a variety of mammals.
Transmits several diseases,
including the 'black death'.

Scorpion fly
Panorpa communis

SIZE AND DESCRIPTION Length 15mm; wingspan 35mm. Head mounted with large eyes, and drawn into a prominent beak, which opens at the tip of the head. Scorpion-like tip to male's abdomen, lacking in female, comprises complex reproductive organs (it is not a sting). Wings are mostly clear, but have many dark spots or patches. Larva resembles a caterpillar. There are several similar species of scorpion fly.

HABITAT Woods, hedgerows and shaded gardens throughout Europe except far north.

FOOD AND HABITS Flies May–August. Although fully winged, adults rarely fly far, spending most of their time crawling on vegetation in damp shady places near water and along hedgerows. They scavenge mainly animal material. Eggs are laid in soil, in which the larvae scavenge.

Male feeding

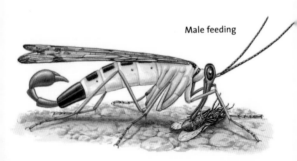

Tail of female

Large Crane-fly
Tipula maxima

SIZE AND DESCRIPTION Length
almost 30mm; wingspan
65mm. Distinctive mottled
brown wings, which are held
at right angles when at rest.
Female has a pointed abdomen,
male a blunted abdomen.
The largest of 300 British
crane-fly species, with a leg
span of 100mm.

HABITAT Found in wooded
areas, including gardens,
in much of Europe.

FOOD AND HABITS Adults fly
April–August. Female lays
eggs in damp mossy
fringes of ponds,
streams and ditches. Larvae
are aquatic, living just below
the water's surface, then
continuing to develop in
submerged leaf litter.

Common Crane-fly
Tipula paludosa

SIZE AND DESCRIPTION Length 25mm. Dark brown along the leading edges of the wings. Female's wings are shorter than her abdomen. Male has a square-ended abdomen, while female's abdomen is pointed, with an ovipositor. Dull brown grub is known as a 'leather-jacket'. Also called Daddy-long-legs.

HABITAT Common in grasslands, parks and gardens in Europe.

FOOD AND HABITS Flies throughout the year, but most numerous in autumn. Adults rarely feed. Female bounces the pointed end of her ovipositor on soil in order to prick it and lay her eggs. Grubs live in the soil and appear at night to gnaw the bases of plant stems.

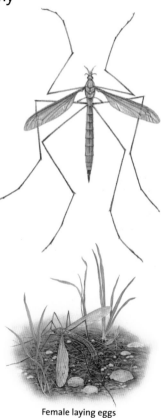

Female laying eggs

Spotted Crane-fly
Nephrotoma appendiculata

SIZE AND DESCRIPTION Length
15–25mm. Largely yellow
abdomen, often with black
spots. Female is larger than
male and has a pointed tip to
her abdomen, while male's
abdomen is clubbed. Wings
are clear and shiny. Fat dark
brown 'leather-jacket' grub.
HABITAT Common on farmland
and in parks and gardens
throughout Europe.
FOOD AND HABITS Flies
May–August. Adults rarely
feed, but grubs feed on roots
and do considerable damage
to garden plants.

Gall Midge
Jaapiella veronicae

Length 2mm. Pointed tip to
abdomen, which is pale yellow.
Wings are hairy. Fine bead-like
antennae. Larvae are tiny and
orange. Inhabits open areas
with small plants. Flies in
swarms on summer evenings,
often entering lighted
windows. Grubs live inside
Germander Speedwell plants
and create hairy galls on the
tips of shoots.

Chironomid Midge
Chironomus plumosus

Length 8mm. Wings are shorter
than the abdomen and held
over the body at rest. Male's
antennae are very bushy. Reddish
aquatic larva is known as a
'bloodworm'. Must have a body
of water in which to lay eggs.
This may be relatively small, for
example a water butt. Adults
rest on walls as they dry out
after emerging from pupae.
Non-biting.

Common Gnat
Culex pipiens

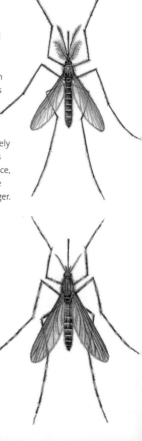

Length 6mm. Wings extend beyond
the abdomen's tip. Female has a
rounded tip to her abdomen. Male
has hairy antennae. Holds abdomen
parallel to the surface on which it is
perching. Aquatic larvae live
beneath the water's surface.
Abundant in Europe. Flies at
night with a monotonous hum. Rarely
bites humans, preferring birds. Eggs
are laid in rafts on the water's surface,
and larvae dangle beneath it. Pupae
swim to the bottom to escape danger.
Adults hibernate in sheds.

Mosquito
Theobaldia annulata

Length 6mm. The largest
mosquito. White rings around
the legs. Dark spots on the wings
formed by convergences of veins.
Widespread where there is
stagnant water for breeding.
Adult females are blood-sucking
and require blood before they
can lay fertile eggs. Males feed
on nectar and other plant juices.
Females hibernate in sheds.

St Mark's Fly
Bibio marci

SIZE AND DESCRIPTION Length 10–12mm. Heavy-looking black fly whose dangling hairy legs add to the impression of a lumbering flight. Female has much larger eyes than male. Larva is primitive with a large head.

HABITAT Gardens, woodland edges and well-vegetated open country throughout Europe.

FOOD AND HABITS Flies late April–May (St Mark's Day is 25 April). Suns itself on walls and flowers. Larvae live beneath the soil, eating rotting material and the roots of plants. Adults feed on nectar.

Fever-fly
Dilophus febrilis

Size and description Length 4mm. Black, but not hairy (compare with St Mark's Fly, page 121). Female has smoky and almost opaque wings, while male's wings are almost clear with a black mark.
Habitat Abundant in most open habitats.
Food and habits Flies March–October, but is most common in spring. Large flocks may cluster on grass stems. Males often hover sluggishly. Larvae live beneath the soil in decaying matter, and may damage living plant roots.

Cleg-fly
Haematopota pluvialis

SIZE AND DESCRIPTION Length 11mm. Dull grey horsefly with a rather cylindrical abdomen. Wings are mottled, and held above abdomen when at rest. Flies silently.

HABITAT Common in May–September, especially in damp woods. Replaced in northern and upland areas by another similar species.

FOOD AND HABITS Flies May–October. Most active in humid and overcast weather. Females are bloodsuckers, biting both humans and livestock. Males drink nectar and plant juices. Larvae live in damp soil, where they prey on other invertebrates.

Window-fly
Scenopinus fenestratus

SIZE AND DESCRIPTION Length 7mm. Small, black and without bristles. Reddish-brown legs, sometimes with black markings. Wings are tightly folded when at rest.

HABITAT Often seen at windows, particularly in old buildings.

FOOD AND HABITS Seems reluctant to fly, apparently preferring to walk away when disturbed. Larvae live in birds' nests and buildings, preying on other insects and their larvae.

Hornet Robber-fly
Asilus crabnoriformis

SIZE AND DESCRIPTION Length 20–30mm. Large and spectacular fly with a stout beak, sturdy legs and a hairy face.

HABITAT Unimproved grassland and heathland in England and Wales. These habitats have been subject to considerable degradation in both range and quality in recent years, as a result of which this robber-fly has experienced a significant decline.

FOOD AND HABITS Flies June–October. Larvae are believed to prey on the larvae of large dung beetles, and adults feed on a variety of insects, including grasshoppers, dung beetles and flies. It therefore requires suitable grassland sward that will support its prey community. Breeds in dung, including cowpats.

Dance-fly
Empis tessellata

SIZE AND DESCRIPTION Length 10–12mm. Dark grey with a small head, pointed and downwards-inclined proboscis, and sturdy thorax. Long hairy legs.

HABITAT Woodland edges, hedges, gardens and open habitats containing shrubs.

FOOD AND HABITS Flies April–August. Hops among hawthorn, daisy and umbellifer flowers. Probes blossoms and hunts for other insects, which it pierces with its proboscis. May be seen on the wing carrying flies it has caught.

Large Bee-fly
Bombylius major

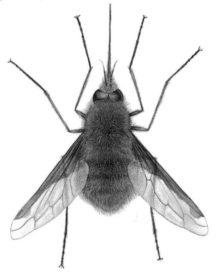

SIZE AND DESCRIPTION Length 10–12mm; wingspan 20–25mm. Brown, furry and bee-like coat, and a long proboscis. Dark leading edges to the wings. Legs are long and slender.

HABITAT Sunny wooded places across Europe, but rare in far north.

FOOD AND HABITS Hovers, using its long front legs to steady itself as it reaches for nectar with its long proboscis. Female drops eggs in flight, and larvae develop as parasites in solitary bee and wasps' nests.

Hover-fly
Rhingia campestris

Length 10mm. Tan coloured,
often with a black line down
the centre of the abdomen,
and a hairy fringe. Looks rather
like a bald bee. Long proboscis.
Occurs in flower-rich habitats
throughout most of Europe.
Adults seen April–November.
Feeds on blue and purple
flowers with deep tubes.
Lays eggs in cow dung.

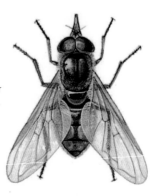

Hover-fly
Syrphus ribesii

Length 10mm. Yellow-and-
black-striped with a rounded
abdomen. Larva is green and
slug-like. There are several
similar species. Found in flower-
rich habitats across Europe.
Flying adults seen March–
November. Males perch on
leaves or twigs up to 2.5m from
the ground and produce a high-
pitched whining song. Feeds
mainly on nectar, but will also
crush and swallow pollen.
Larvae feed on aphids.

Hover-fly
Volucella zonaria

Size and description Length 15–25mm. Abdomen is chestnut at the front, and there are two yellow-orange and black stripes and a brown tinge to the wings near the thorax. Coloration gives it a Hornet-like appearance (it also sounds like a Hornet, page 173).

Habitat Woodland, woodland edges and gardens from Mediterranean to southern England.

Food and habits Flies May–November. Feeds on nectar, pollen and honeydew. Larvae scavenge in wasps' nests.

Hover-fly
Scaeva pyrastri

Length 12–15mm. Black abdomen
with six bold cream crescents.
Rounded abdomen. Slug-like
larva. Occurs in flower-rich
habitats across much of Europe,
but not northern Scandinavia
and rare in Scotland. Adults
seen flying May–November, but
most commonly visible in late
summer. Feeds on nectar
and honeydew. Larvae
feed on aphids.

Hover-fly
Melanostroma scalare

Length 6–9mm. Narrow abdomen
with yellow marks. Male's abdomen
is narrower than female's, which
narrows towards the thorax.
Common in herb-rich areas
and gardens. Flies
April–November. Often
seen on hawthorn
blossoms in May. Larvae
feed on aphids.

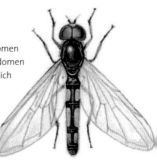

Drone-fly
Eristalis tenax

Length 10–15mm. Looks like a
Honey Bee drone. Dark anvil marks
on abdomen. Larva is called a 'rat-
tailed maggot' because of its long
rear breathing tube. Very common
in parks, gardens and other
flower-rich places across
Europe. Can be seen
throughout the year.
Nectar and pollen eater.
Larvae live in stagnant water,
sewage and dung-hills.

Flesh-fly
Sarcophaga carnaria

Length 12–20mm. Red eyes.
Grey and black chequered
abdomen. Large feet. Often
seen around houses, but
rarely indoors. Found in a
wide range of habitats
throughout Europe. Active all
year round. Feeds as adult on
nectar, rotting carrion and
dung. Females are live-
bearers. Maggots feed on
dung and carrion.

Fruit-fly
Drosophilia funebris

SIZE AND DESCRIPTION Length 3mm. Small dark brown fly. One of many similar species.

HABITAT Widespread in gardens, farms, orchards and food factories.

FOOD AND HABITS Most common in summer and autumn, but present all year in food and drinks factories, and supermarkets. Attracted by rotting fruits, vinegar, wine and other fermenting material. Larvae feed on decaying vegetable matter. Life cycle from egg to adult can be completed in about a week.

Narcissus-fly
Merodon equestris

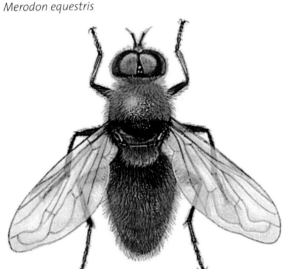

Size and description Length 10–15mm. Bumblebee mimic that has black legs, a prominent bulge on its hindlegs and a hairy brownish-yellow abdomen.

Habitat Gardens, parks, woods and hedges throughout Europe, but not far north.

Food and habits Most common in May, but flies March–August. Eggs are laid in the bases of daffodil bulbs and other bulbs. Larvae burrow down into bulbs.

Common House-fly
Musca domestica

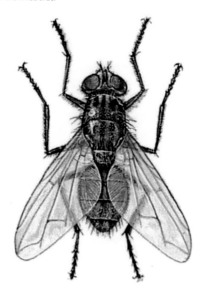

Size and description Length 8mm. Black and tan abdomen.
Habitat In and around houses throughout Europe. Especially
numerous in places where there is plenty of decaying matter.
Food and habits Found during most of the year, but most common
June–September. Does not bite, but favours excrement and thus
carries many disease-causing germs.

Bluebottle
Calliphora vomitoria

Size and description Length 12–15mm. Common blow-fly that has a rounded and hairy metallic blue body. Creamy white larva is carrot-shaped.

Habitat Widespread throughout Europe in many habitats. Often seen in and around houses.

Food and habits Seen all year round, often sunning itself on walls. Female lays eggs on meat and carrion, on which the larvae feed. Male can often be seen on flowers, sipping nectar.

Cabbage Root-fly
Delia radicum

Size and description Length 5–7mm. Bristly black or dark grey abdomen.
Habitat Wherever there are crucifers growing, throughout Europe.
Food and habits Flies March–November, and feeds on nectar. Larvae
feed on the roots of brassicas and Oilseed Rape, causing the leaves
to become limp and yellow.

Greenbottle
Lucilia caesar

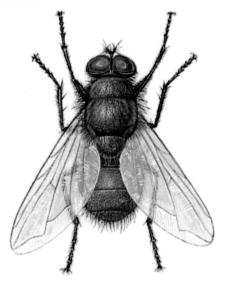

SIZE AND DESCRIPTION Length 8–15mm. Abdomen varies from blue-green to emerald, and becomes coppery with age. Silvery below eyes. One of several metallic green flies.

HABITAT Common around houses but rarely seen indoors. Found in most habitats throughout Europe.

FOOD AND HABITS Adults feed on nectar and carrion juices. Larvae feed on carrion and may be found in wounds on animals.

Yellow Dung-fly
Scathophaga stercoraria

SIZE AND DESCRIPTION Length 10mm. Male is covered with golden-yellow fur. Female is greyish and less furry than male. Both male and female have black antennae.

HABITAT Light woodland and open habitats. Most common in places where there is dung from horses and cows, such as grazing pastures. Found throughout Europe.

FOOD AND HABITS Adults fly for much of the year, preying on other flies on cow dung. Adults develop in cowpats and are abundant on fresh cow dung in summer. Larvae feed on the dung itself.

Celery Fly
Euleia heraclei

SIZE AND DESCRIPTION Length 6mm. Wings mottled dark brown or reddish-brown. Body bulbous.

HABITAT Gardens and open countryside where umbellifers grow. Widespread throughout Europe.

FOOD AND HABITS Flies April–November. Larvae eat the leaves of umbellifers from the inside, causing brownish mines. A serious pest of celery and parsnip.

Thistle Gall Fly
Urophora cardui

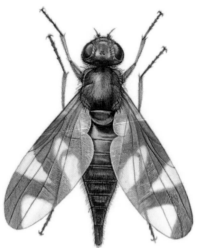

SIZE AND DESCRIPTION Length 7mm. One of several picture-winged flies, with transparent and heavily mottled brown wings that are lighter in female than in male. Female has a prominent pointed ovipositor.
HABITAT Open grassy country where creeping thistles are found. Native to western and central Europe to the Crimea, Siberia and southern Scandinavia at up to 900m elevations.
FOOD AND HABITS Flies May–August. Males claim territories by marking plants with a scent that discourages other males' intrusion. Eggs are laid in creeping-thistle stems, and larvae cause hard egg-shaped galls in the stems. These become buried in litter over winter and are softened by melting snow or spring rain, which stimulates pupation.

Common Carrot Fly
Psila rosae

SIZE AND DESCRIPTION Length 4mm. Black thorax and abdomen, brown legs and a rounded head.

HABITAT Gardens and farmland throughout much of Europe.

FOOD AND HABITS Lays milky-white oval eggs in late spring near young carrots. Cigar-shaped pale yellow larvae infest the roots, often turning them into empty shells.

Stilt-legged Fly
Sepsis fulgens

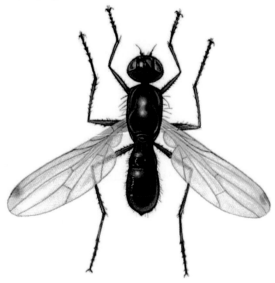

SIZE AND DESCRIPTION Length 3mm. Black with long thin legs. Brown spots on wings. Also called Lesser Dung Fly.

HABITAT Common in open country throughout much of Europe.

FOOD AND HABITS Particularly numerous in autumn, when dense swarms of hundreds of thousands scurry over umbellifers. Hibernates as an adult. Larvae breed in dung. May form large swarms of 30,000–50,000 individuals.

Louse-fly
Ornithomyia avicularia

SIZE AND DESCRIPTION Length 5mm. Greenish legs. Squat brown body
with wings.

HABITAT Found on woodland birds such as owls, pigeons and thrushes.
More frequently found on young birds than on adults, because older
birds preen more effectively.

FOOD AND HABITS Can be seen June–October. Feeds on the blood of
its hosts.

Swallow Louse-fly
Crataerina hirundinis

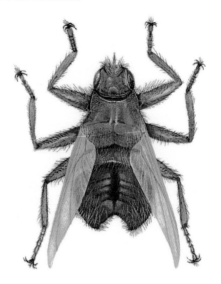

SIZE AND DESCRIPTION Length 5mm. Squat brown body. Flightless with much reduced wings.

HABITAT Nests of Swallows and martins.

FOOD AND HABITS Found on Swallows and martins May–October. Pupae overwinter in the birds' nests and emerge when the birds return in spring.

Green Parasitic Fly
Gymnochaeta viridis

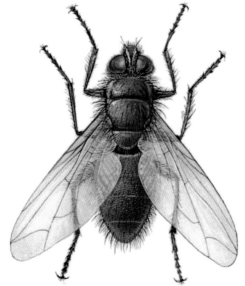

SIZE AND DESCRIPTION Length 10–12mm. Metallic green with hairy brown eyes, abdomen fringed with hairs and bristly legs.

HABITAT Woods, parks and gardens.

FOOD AND HABITS Found on plants March–July. Eggs are laid on plants and the larvae, when small, bore into the larvae of moths.

Stable Fly
Stomoxys calcitrans

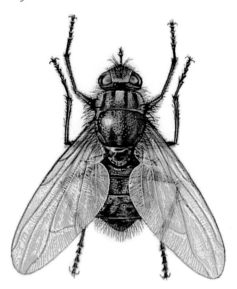

Size and description Length 8mm. Blackish abdomen that is rather short and round. Noticeable proboscis.
Habitat Mainly around stables and farms. Found throughout Europe.
Food and habits Flies April–October. Adults suck blood, using their piercing proboscis. Bites horses, cattle and sometimes humans. Larvae feed in dung and stable litter.

Cluster Fly
Pollenia rudis

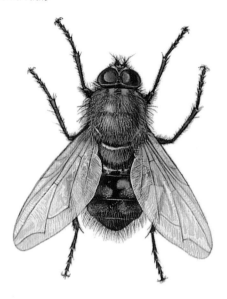

SIZE AND DESCRIPTION Length 8–10mm. Stocky black and grey abdomen.
HABITAT Very common on grassland throughout Europe.
FOOD AND HABITS Flies throughout the year. Feeds on pollen, nectar and
other types of organic matter. Larvae feed on earthworms, in which
they pupate.

Caddis fly
Phryganea grandis

SIZE AND DESCRIPTION Length 20–30mm; wingspan 64mm. Largest caddis fly in Britain. Resembles a small moth with short hairs on the wings. Long antennae are almost the length of the broad dusty-brown wings. Male smaller than female and lacks the black stripe in her forewing. Holds wings over the body like a tent when at rest. One of 198 British species.

HABITAT Slow-moving rivers and streams across most of Europe, but not far south.

FOOD AND HABITS Flies May–November. Feeds on plants and other insect larvae. Flies mostly at night and is attracted to light. Larva makes a protective case up to 50mm long out of pieces of leaf, stones, sand or snail shells (depending on the species). In the species described here, the case is made from spirally arranged cut sections of aquatic leaves, each piece butted to the next. The larva lives in this underwater, dragging it around like a snail's shell. Adults live for about a week.

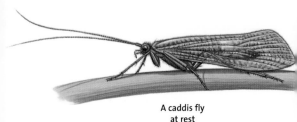

**A caddis fly
at rest**

Larva in
protective case

Gooseberry Sawfly
Nematus ribesii

SIZE AND DESCRIPTION Length to 10mm. Female has a yellow abdomen. Male has a black abdomen and is thinner than female. Larva is green with a black head.

HABITAT Common in gardens throughout most of Europe, but not far north.

FOOD AND HABITS Adults fly April–September. Larvae feed gregariously on the leaves of gooseberries and currants. Pupates in the soil.

Hawthorn Sawfly
Trichiosoma tibiale

SIZE AND DESCRIPTION Length 20mm. Leathery wings, and a hairy abdomen and thorax. Larva is pale green with a brown head.
HABITAT Hedgerows, scrubby places and other habitats with hawthorns throughout northern and central Europe.
FOOD AND HABITS Flies May–June. Larvae feed on hawthorn and spin a tough cocoon in which they pupate and from which the adults bite their way out.

Horntail
Urceros gigas

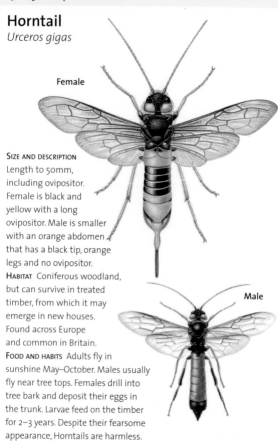

Female

Male

<small>SIZE AND DESCRIPTION</small>
Length to 50mm,
including ovipositor.
Female is black and
yellow with a long
ovipositor. Male is smaller
with an orange abdomen
that has a black tip, orange
legs and no ovipositor.
<small>HABITAT</small> Coniferous woodland,
but can survive in treated
timber, from which it may
emerge in new houses.
Found across Europe
and common in Britain.
<small>FOOD AND HABITS</small> Adults fly in
sunshine May–October. Males usually
fly near tree tops. Females drill into
tree bark and deposit their eggs in
the trunk. Larvae feed on the timber
for 2–3 years. Despite their fearsome
appearance, Horntails are harmless.

Ruby-tailed Wasp
Chrysis ignita

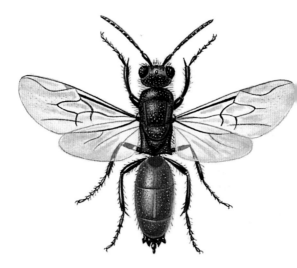

SIZE AND DESCRIPTION Length 7–10mm. Abdomen is brilliant red or purple. Head is blue-green with a golden sheen.

HABITAT Wide range of open habitats, including walls and tree trunks, throughout Europe.

FOOD AND HABITS Adults fly April–September, feeding on nectar. May be seen on walls and tree trunks searching for the nests of mason wasps (page 166) in which to lay eggs. Larvae feed on the grubs of the host and food stored by it.

Yellow Ophion
Ophion luteus

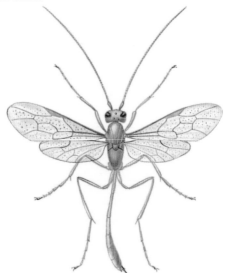

SIZE AND DESCRIPTION Length 15–20mm. Yellowish-brown with a strongly arched abdomen and thorax. Large black eyes. One of about 4,000 European ichneumon flies – parasitic flies that lay their eggs in the larvae of various other insects.

HABITAT Well-vegetated habitats in most of Europe, but not far north.

FOOD AND HABITS Adults fly July–October. Attracted by light. Feeds on nectar and pollen. Eggs are laid in the larvae or pupae of several species, with usually one grub per host. Adult emerges from the host's pupa. Female's ovipositor can deliver a painful jab to humans.

Ichneumon fly
Netelia testacea

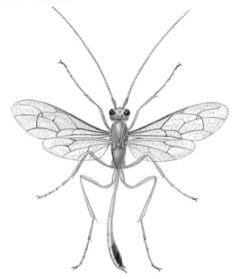

SIZE AND DESCRIPTION Length 17mm. Yellowish-brown with a strongly arched abdomen with a dark tip.

HABITAT Found in well-vegetated habitats throughout much of Europe.

FOOD AND HABITS Flies all summer at night and is attracted to lighted windows. Feeds on the host moth larva from the outside.

Ichneumon fly
Apanteles glomeratus

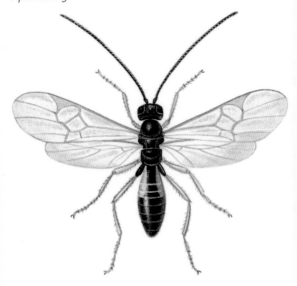

SIZE AND DESCRIPTION Length 3–4mm. Black with smoky wings and brown legs. Larvae are pale brown, small and almost translucent.
HABITAT Occurs throughout Europe in cultivated areas and places where its hosts are found.
FOOD AND HABITS Adults fly in two broods in summer. Eggs are laid in the larvae of Large White (*Pieris brassicae*) and Black-veined White (*Aporia crataegi*) butterflies. Up to 150 grubs emerge inside a larva and devour it, leaving an empty skin.

Ichneumon fly
Pimpla instigator

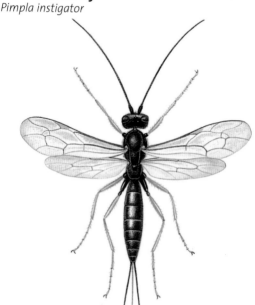

SIZE AND DESCRIPTION Length 10–24mm. Body is black with obvious orange legs. Female's ovipositor is roughly half the length of her abdomen. The most common of the European ichneumon fly species.

HABITAT Most habitats throughout Europe.

FOOD AND HABITS Present all summer. An ectoparasite of moth larvae, especially those of Snout (*Hypena proboscidalis*). The female can inject as many as 150 eggs into a defenceless larva. The grubs grow inside the larva, feeding on its body.

Oak Apple Gall Wasp
Biorhiza pallida

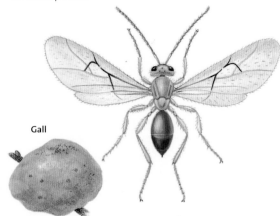

Gall

SIZE AND DESCRIPTION Length 1.7–2.8mm. Small brown wasp. Galls are brownish or reddish, spherical and reach 3–5cm in diameter.

HABITAT Oak trees in many parts of Europe.

FOOD AND HABITS Oak apples appear on oaks in April–May, with each gall containing up to 30 larvae of the sexual generation. A gall often contains only one sex. The adult wasps emerge from the galls in June–July, males appearing a day or two before females. After mating, females deposit their eggs in the rootlets of oaks. The resulting spherical root galls occur in clusters, each gall only about 10mm in diameter and containing a single larva of the asexual generation. The adults – all wingless females – emerge in the second winter. They crawl up the tree to lay eggs in buds in the canopy. These result in oak apple galls and the sexual generation of gall wasps.

Robin's Pincushion
Diplolepis rosae

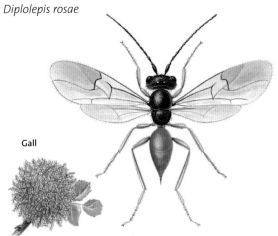

Gall

SIZE AND DESCRIPTION Length 4mm. Small wasp with a black head and thorax, and orange abdomen and legs. Moss-like gall is up to 10cm wide and grows on wild roses. It changes from green, through pink and crimson, to reddish-brown. It is roughly pea-sized, with the hairs attaining a length of up to 35mm. Grub is whitish. Gall is also known as Bedeguar Gall.

HABITAT Open countryside, woodland edges, gardens and parks with Field and Dog Roses.

FOOD AND HABITS Flies April–June. Lays up to 60 eggs in each leaf bud. The asexual wasps emerge in spring. Less than 1 per cent are male, and females lay eggs without mating. Galls mature in autumn.

Common Spangle Gall Wasp
Neuroterus quercusbaccarum

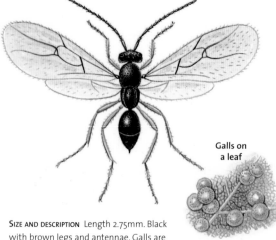

**Galls on
a leaf**

SIZE AND DESCRIPTION Length 2.75mm. Black
with brown legs and antennae. Galls are
brownish circles on the undersides of oak leaves (up to 100 galls are
scattered over the undersurface of a single leaf, giving the impression
of spangling), or small and spherical like currants.

HABITAT Oak trees throughout Europe.

FOOD AND HABITS Galls appear on leaves in late summer. Each contains
a single larva of the asexual generation. In autumn the gall and its
grub drop to the ground. The larvae continue to develop, and the
adults that emerge in February–March are all females. They lay their
eggs in young male catkins without fertilization, resulting in the
'currant' galls of the sexual generation. Adults emerge in summer,
and females lay their eggs on the undersides of leaves.

Red Ant
Myrmica rubra

SIZE AND DESCRIPTION Length
4–5mm (worker). Workers
are chestnut-brown, with
a pedicel (the bead-like
structure formed from
the first abdominal
segments, characteristic
of ants) of two segments.
Males and queens, which
appear in late summer and
early autumn, are about
one-and-a-half times as
long as workers. Males
have longer and less
bulbous abdomens
than females. Red
Ants can sting.
HABITAT Open habitats
throughout Europe.
FOOD AND HABITS Omnivorous,
tending towards animal food.
A Red Ant colony contains one
or more queens and a few
hundred workers.

Black Garden Ant
Lasius niger

SIZE AND DESCRIPTION Length to 5mm (worker). Workers are black or dark brown, with the pedicel in a single segment. Flying ants, which emerge in July and August, are males and females. They are about twice the size of workers. Black Garden Ants do not sting.

HABITAT Open habitats throughout Europe, including gardens.

FOOD AND HABITS Omnivorous, but especially fond of sweet foods and will 'milk' aphids for their honeydew. A colony consists of a queen and several thousand workers. Winged males and females emerge for mating flights in summer. Males die after mating; females break off their wings and seek a suitable nesting site. Birds take a heavy toll of ants during their mating flights. Very few females survive to create new colonies.

An ant's life cycle

Larva

Eggs

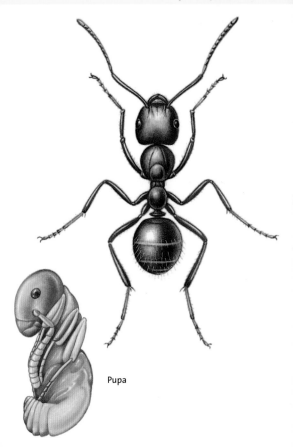

Pupa

Yellow Meadow Ant
Lasius flavus

SIZE AND DESCRIPTION Length to 4mm (worker). Yellowish-brown with a single-segmented pedicel. Males and females fly in July and August, and are about twice the size of workers. The queen is darker. Yellow Meadow Ants do not sting.

HABITAT Orchards and rough grassland throughout Europe.

FOOD AND HABITS Creates the anthills that are a characteristic feature of rough grassland. Mating flocks can be very substantial.

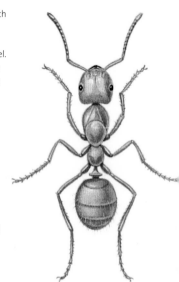

Yellow Lawn Ant
Lasius umbratus

SIZE AND DESCRIPTION Length
4–5mm (worker). Yellowish
with the pedicel in a
single segment.
HABITAT Grassy places
throughout Europe.
FOOD AND HABITS Lives
almost entirely below
ground; usually only seen
when a lawn is dug up.
A parasitic ant species –
the queen finds a worker
ant of the same genus, kills
it to gain its scent and is
then able to enter its nest.
Once inside she finds and
kills the queen. The worker
ants then care for her
larvae, and gradually the
colony becomes one of
Yellow Lawn Ants.

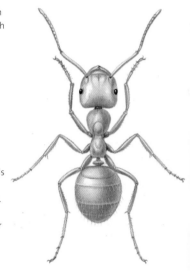

Mason wasp
Ancistrocerus parietinus

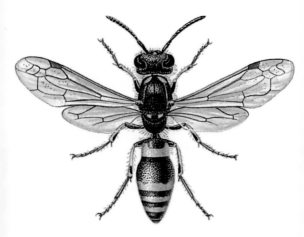

Size and description Length 10–14mm. Black and yellow with a squarish black mark on the first yellow band of its pear-shaped abdomen.

Habitat Common almost everywhere in Europe.

Food and habits Adults fly April–August. Feeds mainly on nectar and honeydew. Female makes a mud nest in a mortar cavity or natural crevice, then stocks the nest with paralysed caterpillars. Is itself parasitised by Ruby-tailed Wasp (page 153).

German Wasp
Vespula germanica

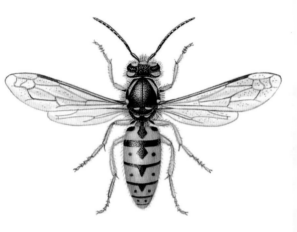

SIZE AND DESCRIPTION Length 12–16mm (worker). Looks very like a Common Wasp (page 168), but has marks on either side of the thorax bulge. Face usually has three black spots. Folds its wings along the sides of its body when resting. Queens are much bigger than workers.

HABITAT Common in most habitats except far north.

FOOD AND HABITS Flies May–October. Hibernating queens can also be seen in winter. Nesting habits are similar to those of Common Wasp, but the nest paper is greyer and less brittle. Nests in holes, which are often in buildings.

Common Wasp
Vespula vulgaris

SIZE AND DESCRIPTION Length 9–18mm (worker). Black and yellow with
four yellow spots at the rear of the thorax. Yellow marks on either side
of the thorax usually have parallel sides.

HABITAT Common in most habitats throughout Europe.

FOOD AND HABITS Lives in annual colonies that are started by a queen,
which lays all the eggs. Usually nests in well-drained underground
sites such as hedgebanks, but also uses cavities in walls and lofts.
Nest is roughly spherical, up to a metre across and covered with shell-
like pieces of yellowish paper. It is made by chewing up fragments of
rotten wood and is quite brittle.

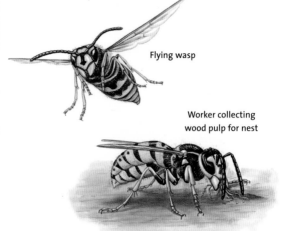

Flying wasp

**Worker collecting
wood pulp for nest**

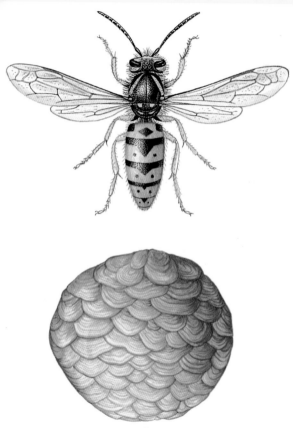

Wasps' nest

Digger wasp
Pemphredon lugubris

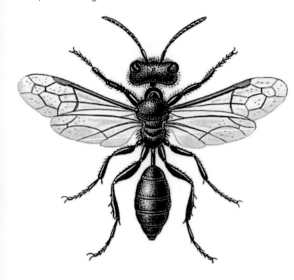

Size and description Length 10–11mm. Black with a finely waisted abdomen and a large squarish head.

Habitat Woodland edges and gardens. Absent from northern Scotland and northern Scandinavia.

Food and habits Flies May–September. Nests in rotting wood, keeping a larder of aphids for the wasp larvae.

Digger wasp
Ectemnius quadricinctus

SIZE AND DESCRIPTION Length 13–14mm. Black and yellow abdomen, a large squarish head and a narrow waist. One of several species of burrowing, usually solitary wasps.

HABITAT Woodland edges and gardens with wood piles throughout central and southern Europe.

FOOD AND HABITS Adults visible June–October. Feeds on pollen and catches flies on umbellifers. Nests in rotting wood, keeping a larder of paralysed insects, particularly hover-flies.

Black Digger Wasp

Trypoxylon figulus

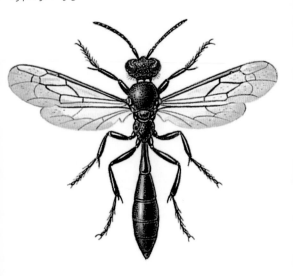

SIZE AND DESCRIPTION Length 6–12mm. Black with a slender tapering abdomen in which segments are clearly visible.

HABITAT Woodland and gardens throughout Europe, but not northern Scotland and northern Scandinavia.

FOOD AND HABITS Flies May–September. Nests in woodworm holes and hollow stems, stocking the brood cells with small spiders for the grubs to feed on.

Hornet
Vespa crabro

SIZE AND DESCRIPTION Length 20–35mm. Largest social wasp in Europe.
Chestnut-brown and gold. Less aggressive than most other wasps.
HABITAT Wooded areas, parks and gardens throughout most of Europe,
but not Scotland, Ireland and northern Scandinavia.
FOOD AND HABITS Nests in hollow trees, wall cavities and chimneys.
Adults favour fruits and sap from damaged trees. Preys on insects
as large as butterflies and dragonflies, which are fed to its young.

Mining bee
Andrena haemorrhoa

SIZE AND DESCRIPTION Length 10–12mm. Dark abdomen with a yellow tip, which is larger in male. Female has a white face, while male's face is pale brown.

HABITAT Woodland edges, scrub and gardens throughout northern and central Europe.

FOOD AND HABITS An early spring species that seeks nectar from Blackthorn, Sallow and Common Dandelion. Solitary species.

Tawny Mining Bee
Andrena fulva

Size and description Length 10–12mm. Female has a bright yellow abdomen, while male, which is smaller, is dark.

Habitat Open habits including gardens, parks and woodland edges. Found throughout central and southern Europe, including southern England.

Food and habits Flies April–June. Nests in the ground, especially on lawns, throwing spoil from the nest hole into a small volcano-like mound. Solitary species.

Mining bee
Andrena hattorfiana

Size and description Length 12–15mm. Dark brown with yellow towards the tip of its abdomen. Largest British species of mining bee.

Habitat Anywhere in southern and central Europe, including southern Britain, where there are flowers as well as soil in which to mine nesting tunnels.

Food and habits Flies June–September. Female collects nectar and pollen in summer to line the cells of her nest. She then lays an egg in each. Young hatch the following spring.

Flower Bee
Anthophora plumipes

Size and description Length 14–16mm. Female is black with hairy legs. Male has a rusty-brown thorax and a darkish tip to his abdomen. Looks like a bumblebee, but has large eyes that reach to the jaws.

Habitat Many well-drained habitats. Common around human settlements. Found in much of Europe, but not Scotland.

Food and habits Flies March–June. Feeds on nectar, using its long tongue to reach into tubular flowers. Nests in soil and soft mortar.

Mason Bee
Osmia rufa

SIZE AND DESCRIPTION Length 8–13mm. Black head and thorax with reddish-brown hair on the abdomen. Female is larger than male, but male has longer antennae. Female has curved bull-like horns between her antennae.

HABITAT Anywhere with flowers and suitable nest-holes across central and southern Europe, including southern England.

FOOD AND HABITS Flies April–July. Nests are in holes, and are composed of several cells of mud.

Honey Bee
Apis mellifera

SIZE AND DESCRIPTION Length 10–15mm; 20mm (queen). Colours vary from dark brown to orange. Can sting, but will rarely do so. An important pollinator that also makes honey.

HABITAT Native of south-east Europe, now found almost everywhere. Recent decline in European populations is probably due to varroa mite infestations, use of insecticides and the increased resistance of various bee pests and diseases.

FOOD AND HABITS Flies spring–late autumn. Lives in colonies with a single queen. These may number 50,000 bees, including a queen, workers (sterile females) and drones (males). Wild colonies usually nest in tree holes. Nests contain combs of hexagonal cells, which are used for rearing grubs and storing pollen and honey.

Buff-tailed Bumblebee
Bombus terrestris

SIZE AND DESCRIPTION Length 20–22mm. Yellow collar and second abdominal segment. Tip of abdomen is buffish-white; queen's abdominal tip is buffish in Britain, but white elsewhere.

HABITAT Common in flowery habitats throughout Europe. Absent from far north.

FOOD AND HABITS Queens emerge April–May; nests produce workers May–August. Nests well below ground level.

White-tailed Bumblebee
Bombus lucorum

SIZE AND DESCRIPTION Length 20–22mm. Yellow collar and second abdominal segment, with white tip to abdomen. Only females of all bumblebee species are capable of stinging; contrary to popular belief, they do not die after doing so.

HABITAT Common in well-vegetated places throughout Europe.

FOOD AND HABITS A very early flier, with queens emerging February–April; nests produce workers May–August. Nests below ground.

Meadow Bumblebee
Bombus pratorum

SIZE AND DESCRIPTION Length 16–18mm. Collar and second abdominal segment are yellow. Tip of abdomen is orange-brown. Colour of this species is quite variable.

HABITAT Well-vegetated habitats across Europe, but not far north. One of the most common bumblebee species.

FOOD AND HABITS Queens emerge March–April; nests produce workers May–August. Very agile, visiting both long tubular flowers and open flowers. Nests on, below or above the ground, including in nest-boxes.

Field Bumblebee
Bombus pascuorum

Size and description Length to 18mm. Can be identified by its reddish-brown thorax (which is darker in the northern part of its range). Thin covering of brownish hairs on the abdomen.

Habitat Occurs in well-vegetated habitats, but not in exposed places. A common bumblebee species.

Food and habits Queens appear April–May; nests produce workers May–August. Colonies live longer into autumn than those of other bumblebee species. Nests in old birds' nests, nest-boxes and long grasses at ground level.

Garden Bumblebee
Bombus hortorum

SIZE AND DESCRIPTION Length 20–24mm. Collar, rear of thorax and first segment of the abdomen are yellow. Tip of the abdomen is whitish.
HABITAT Prefers open areas rich in the flowers of plants such as vetches, clovers and nettles. Found throughout Europe, including Britain. A common bumblebee species.
FOOD AND HABITS Queens emerge May; nests produce workers late May–August. Queens often seen on White Dead-nettle. Nests on or just beneath the ground.

Violet Carpenter Bee
Xylocopa violacea

SIZE AND DESCRIPTION Length 20–30mm. Big bee with a hairy violet-black body and violet-blue-tinted wings. Male has a yellowish stripe near the tips of his antennae. Not aggressive and rarely stings.
HABITAT Common in central and southern Europe, and moving north. In Britain it is breeding in Leicestershire.
FOOD AND HABITS Flies fast and comes to flowers for nectar. Female makes a nest in dead wood, and may make three in her lifetime. Adults spend winter in holes in trees or walls.

Leaf-cutter Bee
Megachile centuncularis

SIZE AND DESCRIPTION Length 10–12mm. Dark above, but female has an orange pollen brush under her abdomen.

HABITAT Woods, gardens and parks throughout Europe, but not far north.

FOOD AND HABITS Flies May–August, visiting a range of flowers. Female uses her jaws to cut elliptical or round sections from the leaves and petals of roses and other plants. The leaf pieces are then used to make sausage-shaped cells for the bee grubs in the bee's nest cavity, which is usually in wood.

Wool Carder Bee
Anthidium manicatum

SIZE AND DESCRIPTION Length 11mm. Thorax is black. Abdomen is black with yellow marks on either side. Legs are yellow. Not very hairy. Male is notably larger than female.

HABITAT Woodland edges, parks, gardens and hedgerows containing appropriate nest-lining material and nest-holes. Widespread throughout Europe except far north.

FOOD AND HABITS Flies June–August. Female collects hairs from plants, then carries them rolled in a ball beneath her body to the nest-hole in timber or masonry.

Cuckoo bee
Psithyrus campestris

Size and description Length 15–17mm. Thorax has yellowish hairs behind the head and grey hairs in front of the abdomen, which is largely shiny and hairless. Variable in colour – dark form widespread, and more common among males than females; very pale form occurs in western Scotland. Male is also smaller than female. Does not look like its host bumblebee species. As a cuckoo bee, there are no pollen baskets on its hindlegs.

Habitat Most habitats, but avoids exposed places. Occurs throughout Europe, but not Scotland and northern Scandinavia.

Food and habits Emerges late spring. Parasitises Field Bumblebee (page 183), laying eggs in its nest that the bumblebee then looks after.

Cuckoo bee
Psithyrus barbutellus

SIZE AND DESCRIPTION Length 20mm. Resembles Garden Bumblebee (page 184), but is less hairy. The black abdomen has a white tip. No pollen baskets on the hindlegs.

HABITAT Gardens, parks and open country across Europe. In Britain not found in Shetland, and elsewhere widespread but often not common, even in south.

FOOD AND HABITS Emerges late spring. Parasitises Garden Bumblebee by laying eggs in the nest, often killing the queen. The bumblebee workers then rear the cuckoo bee's grubs as if they had been laid by the original queen.

Index

Scientific names